Escape Average

Escape Becoming Average
After College Graduation

~

[ESC][AVG]

Rob Sakalas

Library of Congress Cataloging-in-Publication Data:
Sakalas, Rob
Escape Average: [ESC][AVG] Escape Becoming Average after
  College Graduation / Rob Sakalas.
    p. cm.
ISBN-13: 979-8-9897898-0-1

Printed in the United States of America.

Table of Contents

Preface   5

Chapter 1 | What is [ESC][AVG] and Why Should I Care?   7

Chapter 2 | Your Grand "Do-Over"   16

Chapter 3 | Not Fair, but Get On With It   21

Chapter 4 | Launch Angle and the Domino Effect   23

Chapter 5 | Choose your Destiny, Daily   29

Chapter 6 | Habits and Designing your own Operating System   36

Chapter 7 | Finding True North   43

Chapter 8 | Opportunities are Often Disguised as Hard Work   52

Chapter 9 | Leverage the Greatest Technology — Pale Ink   56

Chapter 10 | First Downs and your Number One Priority   60

Chapter 11 | Taming the Dragon   64

Chapter 12 | Consciously Differentiate   68

Chapter 13 | Unstoppable Force of Nature   72

Chapter 14 | Creative Idea Hero   75

Chapter 15 | Give the Gifts that Matter   78

Chapter 16 | Years to Build, Seconds to Lose   80

Chapter 17 | Work Harder on Yourself than on Your Job   85

Chapter 18 | Red Pill Clarity and Time   93

Chapter 19 | Invent, Innovate, Initiate   99

Chapter 20 | Nothing Ventured, Nothing Gained   103

Chapter 21 | No Gold Medal for Starting the Race   110

Chapter 22 | Stay Curious and Become a Critical Thinker   115

Chapter 23 | The WD-40 of Success   119

Chapter 24 | Don't Forget the Super Glue   124

Chapter 25 | Be Mindful of your Inner Circle   129

Chapter 26 | The 'Why' Matters Most, but Plan It Too   132

Chapter 27 | Defeating the Stress Hairball   137

Chapter 28 | Health is Usually not Accidental   143

Chapter 29 | Taking the Reins   147

Chapter 30 | Don't Swim Upstream   151

Chapter 31 | Swinging for the Fence   156

Chapter 32 | What Gets Measured Gets Improved   160

Chapter 33 | Surfing the Banzai Pipeline   163

Chapter 34 | Expectations are Far from Benign   168

Chapter 35 | The Ultimate Secret Catalyst   171

Chapter 36 | Competence Required   175

Chapter 37 | Confident and Calm Under Pressure   177

Chapter 38 | Embrace the Good Stuff   179

Chapter 39 | Why Not You?   181

Acknowledgements   183

Preface

Welcome. I am delighted that you are here.

You can be the hero of your own story, achieving greatness. The first step is deciding to become great, deciding to not settle for becoming average. The second step is seriously figuring out what success is for you, because that definition varies greatly from person to person. After that, you must build habits that will get you to your targets.

Becoming a top 10%er is worth the effort, worth the discipline and sacrifices required. Unfortunately, many graduate from college without much guidance and coaching. Others squander their time, unaware of the ramifications of wasting years. It's one thing to be certain that the world is going to be your oyster. It's another to set the real-world on fire and accomplish your most ambitious goals.

It really helps to have a plan.

Many college grads have families that are well-intentioned, but they don't know much about the world of business and therefore give little in the way of helpful guidance. Many don't have any mentors who understand the Fortune 500 or Wall Street, or what it means to start out in a high-end professional career. Another less-than-helpful reality is that a great many graduates do not want to have deep conversations with family because that scenario invariably feels all too judgmental and devolves into hard feelings and arguments.

This book will help you get off to a great start and keep first things first, for the coming decades. It will help you accomplish more, help you avoid mistakes, it will save you time, and it will help you make better decisions. It will help you create a great plan and, ultimately, help you escape average.

Be the hero you were born to be.

Chapter 1 | What is [ESC][AVG] and Why Should You Care?

After a lot of thrashing around, after dropping too many classes, after too many hard-to-understand teaching assistants, and after changing your major, you have graduated. All those late nights, all those distractions, all those less-than-stable friends begging you to drink yet another tequila shot, all those questionable decisions that you now mostly regret, in the end, didn't derail you. Woo-hoo.

Congratulations!

Welcome to the real world. The real world is relentless. It is a *'great job, now, what have you done for me lately'* world, and the graduation fanfare is now in the rearview mirror. At this moment, the real world simply doesn't care about you.

As it turns out, you have a monumentally important, highly personal decision to make. You must answer this question: *Do you want to be average in your life?* The sooner you decide with all-in commitment that you will escape average, the better off you will be.

You might think this isn't a decision you have to make now but it absolutely is. The real world doesn't care if you flourish or stumble along, how you bolt out of the starting gate, or what new habits you create. Those habits — good or bad — will either elevate your trajectory, land you in the middle of the herd, or crash your life.

Does anyone set out to become average? Does anyone want to be average? Do you?

The answer is no. You want to become a top 10%'er. It's perhaps a little scary to think about, however. You really want to be a top 1% type, but first things first, as you realize that a lot of stuff, some of which is out of your control, must fall into place for that top 1% outcome. Bill Gates had a lot of luck and help along the way.

The truth is no one wants to be average, but, by definition, most people are within one standard deviation of average, the 70% in the middle hump of the bell curve. Consider this: In a survey published in the Journal of Applied Social Psychology, researchers asked people how they rate themselves on a scale of 1-10 in terms of driving a car. Nearly everyone decided that they were at least a 7 or better[1]. No one wants to be average, and in fact, perceive themselves through a biased, all-too-positive lens.

The good news is that there's a formula to escape average. It's not easy to follow and execute, but it is not mission impossible. It requires accurately perceiving yourself, your strengths and weaknesses, and the surrounding world. It takes building great habits, developing the right attitude, and avoiding some predictable pitfalls. Above all, it requires making the right, smart choices while taking some chances.

This book will show you the formula – abbreviated as [ESC][AVG] – to become a top 10%'er.

Early in life, long before college graduation, in a moment of outstanding clarity, I decided that I desperately wanted to be above average at everything. The good news is mostly I pulled it off — but wow — I made a lot of mistakes, learned a lot of lessons, took some painful detours, wasting years of time. I realized that there is a lot of stuff I wish I knew when I was twenty-two. All those lessons, tips, and life hacks are in this book: it will help you avoid some of the mistakes, take better advantage of opportunities, see straight, make good decisions, and ultimately escape "average" sooner than you would without it.

Why escape average?

Being average is so, well, average. If you remember your statistics class so many beers, margaritas, and spiked seltzers ago, 70% of people land in the fat middle of the bell curve. In America, that group is about 231 million out of 350 million people. In Europe, that group is 550 million and in China, it is over a billion humans. Here is the inescapable fact: The world we live in, a world that is dominated by supply and demand — does not reward average people handsomely — it never has and it never will.

Success is more than income — always remember that — but income is easy to measure. On that one aspect alone, median US individual income in 2021 was approximately $71K[2]. A top 10% income, on the other hand, is a bit more than 3X that, right around $240K depending on which survey you consult[3]. It is good to strive for the top 10%.

There is good news. There has been a remarkable change in societies in just the last 75 years — upward mobility has never been more available and fluid. There are now hundreds of thousands of rags-to-riches stories. Education is more readily available and social media connects people and businesses quickly and efficiently. While the family that you were born into can make a difference, it matters less than ever. The meritocracy and equality trends are accelerating.

Fluid meritocracy means that for every 100 fellow graduates who know you well enough to greet you by name, odds are good that several will become top outliers in terms of success. While ~90% earn a high school diploma, ~35% graduate from college with a bachelor's degree by the time they are 25 years old[4]. Just being a graduate gives you a greater number of career opportunities so it also makes you an odds-on favorite to be in the top third of the broader population; therefore, it is safe to assume that around a dozen of your current acquaintances are likely to become top 10%'ers and a few might just achieve extraordinary top 1% success.

Why not you?

The cold-hard truth is it absolutely, positively can be you, because the rules of success dramatically pivot after the commencement speech, right after people stop saying congratulations. Twenty-two years old — or twenty-three or twenty-four — ushers in a brand-new ball game that you and your comrades have never played before. The truth is most will not play the game the best way possible, but you can, if you want to escape average.

Everything that you practiced and slaved over at school, the book-smart IQ that got you A's or B's in Calculus and Physics, matters far less in the post-grad-universe EQ-dominated world. What is EQ? It is your Emotional (Intelligence) Quotient, and it really matters. EQ is all about understanding and relating to people, not just books and exams. Going forward, the rules by which your efforts will be evaluated, promoted, and compensated are nuanced shades of gray, surrounded by a misty fog, not the black and white, right answer or wrong answer existence that you have known for your first twenty-something years of life.

This 180-degree pivot offers brilliant news: By the end of these next few hours of reading, you will have a handle on the "real world" that exists on the far side of the commencement event. [ESC][AVG] offers lessons on the "right way" to launch into the post-grad universe on a great trajectory for success. Granted, life is not black and white, so there are several "right ways" but, unless someone has a great mentor who he or she consults frequently and really listens to, few of your fellow grads will realize how different the game is, or what matters most to playing it well.

Here's a fundamental truth of the real-world: The "launch angle" of the first few post-grad years of your career have a tremendous effect on your long-term ultimate success. Many young adults throw away the opportunity to launch well, with vision, boldness, and determination.

Many twenty-somethings make excuses and in doing so, stunt their own growth and their own destiny. Henry Ford's great quote is still true today: *"Whether you think you can, or think you can't, you are right."* More than half of your graduating friends have already mentally shot themselves in the foot before getting started and are dropping off the pace. The real-world is the Ironman triathlon with a few Ninja Warrior obstacle courses thrown in along the way and you don't want to start out limping during the first mile with a bad start.

What if you are 29 today, as you read this, and not 22? It is never too late to get on the better path. The longer you wait to launch, the harder it becomes. Hopefully you had a lot of fun in your twenties. You are better off starting today than waiting another five years.

In career-life in the real-world, you don't have to be a genius. Few C-Suite execs of the Global 2000 companies are geniuses, yet each is in the top 99th percentile of career success. Every one of them have a group of sky-high IQ types working for them in their organizations. You clearly don't have to get a perfect score on a college entrance exam when you are 12 years old or play a flawless Beethoven Piano Concerto no. 3 in C minor at 14, to win at the game of life. Although there will always be a few geniuses who knock it out of the park, we find a broad spectrum of people excel, a wild sprinkling of all types, including dropouts, kids from humble or difficult beginnings, even some with handicaps and learning disabilities to overcome.

You might be wondering *"why should I target 'just' escaping average?"* — why not target being in the 99th percentile or even higher than that?

Shooting for the stars is great, but the path for this journey lacks a magic wand that transports you from average to extraordinary in the blink of an eye. Sure, the summit of any endeavor, career, job, or pursuit is often a great neighborhood to be in. But make no mistake: you must build up to it over time. Steve Jobs observed *"If you look closely, most overnight successes took a really long time."* To go from average to fantabulous, you must put in the time, the effort, and the hard work.

There are a multitude of dimensions to escaping average. The first ones that many people think of are money and fame, but there are so many more in life. Few artists are artists for the paycheck. Few doctors are doctors just to join the exclusive country club. The universe sometimes rewards greatness financially, but other times, the rewards come in different ways. [ESC][AVG] will help you in whatever dimensions of success that you decide to pursue.

Escaping average is well within reach of every college graduate, if you follow the formula of [ESC][AVG], because most people will not have the needed discipline, the right attitude, and the grit to live it daily. Once you escape average, attaining top 10% or top 5% success becomes a likely next goal. From there, it becomes possible to attain top 3%, and top 2%, and then top 1%, but each sliver of greater success requires habitualized disciplines and several external factors that work out in your favor. I have never met a self-made top 1%'er who doesn't admit the role "a fortunate series of events or lucky moments" played in breaking through. The Top 1% requires doing it right, plus planets aligning as well. Life doesn't magically teleport anyone from being a 50% average person to top 1%, no matter if we are talking about stand-up comedy, or sculpture, or YouTube influencer, or financial wealth, unless you find a meteor made of diamonds in your backyard. That's about as likely as winning the Powerball Lottery.

The First Question

Here is one of the most important questions that you must answer soon: What does success really mean to you?

For the wise, success is not solely defined by income or wealth. The answer most young adults on the launch pad gravitate to is "money and fame" but the real answer is nuanced and different for all. As you bring your own answer into focus, you must consider what you are willing to give up to achieve your number-one-priority.

Here's a quick reality check. It is undoubtedly easier to achieve a large investment account and financial wealth if you decide to live unusually frugally, say 50% below your means, spend money only on essentials, purchase five-year-old well-cared-for Toyotas, while forgoing modern housing in top metro, most entertainment, getting married, and having kids. Facing those trade-offs, most people try to find a better-balanced target for success.

This little book offers the framework, the methods, the right way, that will help you achieve above average success, through the lens of mistakes I made or witnessed first-hand and the lessons that they taught. I will do my best to share, not preach, as I realize that there is always more to learn. Because of my experiences, many of the examples in [ESC][AVG] will come from the world of big business, sales meetings, and office politics, but the lessons offered often apply to people in many different walks of life. An architect starting her own firm, a realtor building her client base, or a nurse working at Medical City will absolutely find value.

Another big truth of the real-world: Unless you know where you are trying to go, you have no chance of getting there. Defining what success is to you is a complicated question that each person must seriously reconsider and adjust every year. Perspectives evolve, circumstances change, and new doors of opportunity appear as time marches on.

In addition to helping you identify your success definition and targets, this book outlines around thirty ideas, techniques, and disciplines that a person must practice, perfect, and forge into indelible habits, until they become part of his or her core mental operating system, in order to greatly improve the odds of above average success.

Karate offers an excellent way to visualize the process. As you grow and learn in karate, you are taught forms that you practice and practice until the moves become second nature. When your opponent punches with his right hand with an upper-cut to your chin, these now nearly automatic forms or learned habits help you block the punch while keeping your balance and looking for an opportunity to counter-punch. Over time, the right thing to do, the right way to react no matter what the opponent throws at you, becomes a habit, becomes second nature.

[ESC][AVG] elements can be thought of as mental karate. The thirty disciplines of the [ESC][AVG] are similar to the forms black belt candidates practice. You must practice and perfect each one. The primary techniques to use are planning, visualization, and habitualization. Once you have them locked in, once they become second nature, you are ready to react in the most positive way, no matter what mental punch life throws at you and your psyche. Remember this key truth of the real-world: *Life is 10% what happens to you, and 90% how you choose to react to it.* These techniques help you always react the best way possible.

Not everyone who studies [ESC][AVG] will adopt, practice, and perfect all thirty mental disciplines, but it is not time wasted. Perfecting just some of them, perhaps half of them, will virtually guarantee that you will, at a minimum, escape average. Not everyone becomes an outlier high-end blackbelt in karate either.

Before plunging in, consider finding a notebook to use while reading [ESC][AVG]. Many believe that thinking, while writing on paper, is far better than thinking only in your head and studies have shown that retention is at least three times better when you jot notes with a pen. Ideas magically knit themselves together when you see your own notes. I'd suggest a nice Moleskine notebook that you can dedicate to notes-while-reading, so that it is always available for your thoughts and observations throughout the rest of this book and other books too. New ideas magically surface when reading, and it is best not to lose them.

A great mantra to adopt:

All I knew was that I never wanted to be average.
     — Michael Jordan, The GOAT of the NBA

Notes:

1 – https://www.psychologicalscience.org/news/motr/when-it-comes-to-driving-most-people-think-their-skills-are-above-average.html and
Roy, M. M., Liersch, M. J. (2014). I am a better driver than you think: examining self-enhancement for driving ability. Journal of Applied Social Psychology, 43(8), 1648–1659. DOI: 10.1111/jasp.12117

2 – https://www.bankrate.com/personal-finance/median-salary-by-age/ (2021 figures)

3 – https://ofdollarsanddata.com/what-is-considered-rich/ (2022 figures)

4 – Per Wikipedia article regarding educational attainment: "https://en.wikipedia.org/wiki/Educational_attainment_in_the_United_States"

Chapter 2 | Your Grand "Do-Over"

There is a huge difference, a mind-boggling Grand-Canyon-like chasm, between the rules of the game while in school and the rules of the game during your career. While true of virtually every career, it is further complicated by the ever-present political dynamics within larger companies. All companies have politics, but the larger the company, the more complex the landscape.

Believe it or not, this is great news for you, unless you happen to be the valedictorian graduating Summa Cum Laude from an Ivy League institution like Harvard, Yale, or Dartmouth.

Imagine that your life to the point of graduation has been the Olympics. Throughout your academic years, you were like an alpine ski racer in the winter games. In most classes, what mattered most was getting the right numeric grade on each exam, and most questions on each exam usually had a distinct 'right' answer. In essence, few professors cared how you 'looked' going down the mountain, just as long as you passed the correct side of each gate and finished in the right amount of time. If you were one of the fastest down the racecourse, you got an A, while the average skier got a C or B minus.

On the real-world side of the commencement chasm, you will find that you have suddenly become a gymnast in the summer Olympics, competing on the floor exercise. While there are a few compulsory guidelines that must be accomplished during the routine to prove your competence, judges play the pivotal role in evaluating the technical and artistic merits of your routine. Your showmanship, your presentation, your music and choreography, the smallest of details, the reaction of the audience, all matter when tenths of a point separate gold medal winners from the rest of the field.

In the real-world, there is one additional but important distinction when compared to the Olympic Games: most often, the judges are not paying attention to your performance, as their offices are in different cities, they are working on their pet projects, each judge has different priorities, pressures, and distractions, and they often are mostly concerned with their own pay, bonuses, promotions, opportunities, and family issues. When Simone Biles put in her gold medal winning performance on the floor exercise in Rio De Janeiro in August of 2016, she didn't have to worry that the judges were checking their emails, sending texts, and checking the value of their stock portfolio during her performance.

You can't plunge into real-world only using the rules college has taught you and hope to escape average. From an employer's point of view,

1. College was a test to prove you have enough smarts and have enough persistence to put up with enough bullsh*t to survive and eventually thrive at their company.

2. If your college did its job, it helped you develop internal frameworks for learning medium-to-hard stuff in quicker than average time.

3. College should have helped you become a proficient communicator, both verbally and in writing.

4. Colleges universally strive to give you enough mathematics to survive within the real-world.

5. Usually, college gives you a vocabulary and basic understanding of your chosen field, so that when you get a job, you can decipher what the heck coworkers and managers are talking about.

6. Some colleges manage to give you experience with collaborating and working in teams, although this is not universally true.

7. The best colleges, or more accurately the best teachers, open your eyes to the difference between knowledge, understanding, and imagination. If all we needed were facts, "Google It" or "ChatGPT It" would be your entire job description. Imagination is a realm that few truly master, yet that is where the home runs wait for you.

Except for a few careers that are highly specialized such as Nursing and Petroleum Engineering, the skills from school are only a start. You will learn how to actually do your job, on the job. Unlike school, the real-world tends to give you the exam first, then the lesson comes afterwards.

So what is so different on the other side of the chasm?

Emotional intelligence becomes as important or more important than standard IQ. In the real-world where there are few truly right or wrong answers, understanding and being able to control your own emotions, while understanding the emotions of others becomes paramount.

Most university students focused exclusively on their own personal bubble, doing what was needed to get the grade, or land a date to a party. In the real-world, you must become Sherlock Holmes with a great memory, focused on discerning who wants what, from whom, and most importantly, why they want it.

After graduating, my career started at a Fortune 500 firm in high-end professional selling of computer systems. I was fortunate, as my manager Bruce turned out to be a 6'7" emotional intelligence Yoda, a master professional at the art of selling the big deal. I got lucky again, as Bruce took me under his wing and was a proactive mentor. I distinctly remember sitting in his office during the first weeks of my employ as seasoned account managers paraded in and out, discussing the engagements that they were working on. Bruce asked lots of open-ended questions about each customer's emotions and state-of-mind such as 'who does John want to impress?' or 'what's in it for Nancy' or 'who could sabotage the purchase and why.' In just my first month, I quickly realized that the post grad business-world was completely different from the school-world I had just left, where the problems usually had distinct right answers and finding those answers was in my own control. It was a shock to the system, but most new hires don't gain this insight right away, because few are blessed with an EQ masterclass month one.

There are layers of emotional complexity in business and all life's roles, of course. Level One of the emotions dimension is to know thyself. You must first know yourself and master your own emotions. A career path can blow up in a hurry if you hurl a notebook at the wall in frustration during a meeting, or if you pick a fight that can't be won, or if you hold grudges.

Getting to Level Two and Three is crucial to successfully leaping over the commencement chasm. Level Two is accurately observing, understanding, and influencing other people's thoughts and emotions (EQ) on a first-person basis. This is a bit like mastering chess. You must think ahead and there is always more to learn. It helps to jot down your impressions in your secure ideas and observations repository — your *'permanotes'* to coin a new word — because memory fades over time, and often, people with whom you are in contact move on to new assignments, only to crop back up in the future.

Building and maintaining trust is of utmost importance. If people don't trust you, they will hide clues that could have helped you understand them better. You will not master the Level Two Emotional Quotient (EQ) or Level Three Social Quotient (SQ) without trust.

If Level Two is like chess, then Level Three is three-dimensional chess. Understanding the relationships and complex neural network of influence across an organization and the multitudes of people you may never meet firsthand, requires noticing, remembering, and evaluating scant clues. This social intelligence quotient or SQ is an arena that less than 5% master, especially in their first years with a company, but SQ matters tremendously. Barriers exist for the newbie in their career. It is difficult to build insider-like connections when you have not yet achieved trust with a lot of colleagues and therefore have few levers to pull.

If you were in a fraternity or sorority, you have experienced a microcosm for EQ and SQ. If you tried to become an officer, you had to network and try to influence the result. Now, just imagine a world where people are far more separated than one campus, and each one, in some way, is trying to advance or at least remain secure in their employment. Everyone goes home at night to their own families, and often, most people don't know others on the team. At many companies, the culture has scant camaraderie. It is a tricky world.

EQ and SQ define the chasm that must be overcome. In most knowledge-work careers in the post-graduation universe, emotional and social intelligence matter more than figuring out the flow rate of chemicals in a pipe, no disrespect to the engineers who solve difficult math. Even the hard-core engineers realize that getting the optimal answers to pipeline flow still won't land the raise and the promotion. People's relationships matter more, even within right-and-wrong answer science and engineering career paths.

Throughout [ESC][AVG], I will suggest additional materials for those that want to delve deeper on a topic. While most people would refer you to the bestseller _Emotional Intelligence_ by Daniel Goleman, consider the less renown but well-written book by Justin Bariso EQ _Applied: The Real-World Guide to Emotional Intelligence_. It will give you good ideas about putting EQ into action.

Chapter 3 | Not Fair, but Get On with It

While in school, moments happened when you cried "not fair" if not verbally, then inside your head. These moments were few, but they were painful.

In the post-grad universe, not-fair moments happen more often. People with promising momentum get transferred to a different manager that sucks the life out of them. The VP, who was your internal mentor, takes an early retirement or jumps to another company. The one great project that you really hoped to work on gets assigned to Ashley. Your co-worker lies about you and they believe him in a classic he-said she-said no hard proof scenario.

One of the worst "not fair" scenarios is the behind-the-scenes Darth Vader moment. There are always hidden Darth Vaders. You may never meet him or her. Darth will have heard of you second hand, and based on one impression, or one lie, or one politically motivated musing, he or she will have an outsized effect on your career. It pays to look for, connect with, and positively impress the Darths, but there are no guarantees you will find each one, or connect with him or her in time.

Evaluations are often few and far between, and rarely objective. Because of this, even an outstanding personal evaluation disappears as almost no one sees your personnel file unless bad things are happening and those in power are deciding if they will press the ejection-seat button. Few managers fight tooth and nail for their own people, all too often blaming an employee when something goes wrong, usually behind closed doors so that you don't even realize that you took a reputational torpedo with the Senior VP. The SVP typically never asks for your side of the story because he trusts the VPs that report to him.

The real-world is not a world where good grades matter. Too often, no one "grades" anything. First impressions, second impressions, and hearsay make a crucial difference in your attempt to rise in influence, power, stature, brand, and reputation. People being people, they look for people to blame and they remember the bad moment far longer than the good moment, for that is hard-wired in human nature.

In short, the real-world is hard and it is not fair. There are always a few golden colleagues that enjoy protection and gain introductions from a high-placed mentor or connection. Everyone is looking for leverage and trying to stay clear of shrapnel when projects blow up.

The actor Matthew McConaughey summed it up this way: *"Life is not fair. It never was, it is not now, and it won't ever be. Don't fall into the trap, the entitlement trap of feeling like you're the victim. You are not."*

In this not-fair world, there is great opportunity. Sh*t happens. Don't moan, or whine, or blame. A lot of people stew for far too long when they get hit between the eyes by an undeserved haymaker. The soaring few, the above average, get over it, get on with it, truly learn a lesson that they will not repeat, adapt, and decide to stay enthusiastic anyway. All too often a bad moment feels personal, but in business, you often get screwed, and it is usually not personal. Even if it is personal, you must see past all that and realize that life works out best for the people who get on with it and make the best of the situation.

Chapter 4 | Launch Angle and the Domino Effect

The real-world is an emotional, social, and political mess. It is not fair. It can be hard. This is not a reason for depression because this difficult mess offers you opportunity. You can win this game, while plenty of others will have their passion and enthusiasm beat out of them. [ESC][AVG] will help illustrate how you can think straight, what to perfect, and how to launch well.

Where and how you launch matters a heck of a lot.

Most of us don't have the Bill Gates option. After super-early-adopter experience with personal computers while still in high school, at the dawn of the PC age, Bill attended Harvard as a national merit scholar with a near perfect SAT score, later dropping out to pursue his passions around microcomputers. At that point, his options of mainstream employment were quite limited, but his family had enough money and enough belief in Bill to fund his startup. It didn't hurt that Bill befriended key contributors Paul Allen and Steve Ballmer, both brilliant and driven in their own rights, while in school.

Unless your planets align, starting a well-funded venture at 22 is not an option. You must work with what is possible. For most graduates, the best option is often a paying job at an existing company, although if you have a great idea and business plan, pitching to get some angel investors is not a bad thing to try, odds be damned; all that they can say is no. [ESC][AVG] helps no matter which path you choose.

If you choose traditional employment, your available career options are a result of a matrix of factors such as the:
- reputation of the school from which you graduated,
- supply and demand for candidates with your degree,
- fit of your degree for open positions,
- quality of your personal network,

- willingness of your contacts to actively share their network with you,
- sheer number of positions that you apply for,
- your grade point average,
- how professional and outstanding your resume is,
- your personality and ability to make a great first impression and sell yourself,
- your effort and persistence in the pursuit of interviews and alternative ways in,
- the number of interviews where you over-prepare, things click, and you excel, and
- even a bit of luck.

Please don't have any false illusions. A Summa Cum Laude graduate from Yale or Stanford will have a broader range of opportunities than you. Once employed, she will have greater instant credibility as a young employee. Her odds are better than yours, but she has no guarantees either. Conversely, the number of opportunities available to a community college graduate who recently emigrated from a foreign land are significantly more limited than they are for you, but still, there is a possibility for our newbie to excel. Modern western society is more fluid and upwardly mobile than ever in history.

No matter how many options you can generate, it will always come down to making the best choice that you can. How do you choose?

There is a matrix of key aspects that differentiates one company as a better choice over another, including leadership in their industry, revenue and earnings growth, staying power, brand value, their belief in meritocracy, and more. Additionally, smaller aspects matter a lot, such as the specific manager you would work for, the quality of the training, the culture, the policies that govern promotions, and more. You do not want to volunteer for a cutthroat place where they simply throw you in the deep end and see if you sink or swim, nor is going to work for a place that promotes only based on how many years you have been there.

The best path is to land at a leading company with a great brand that is growing quickly — a good yardstick would be organic revenue growth of at least 10% per year for the last few years. Organic growth is growing company sales without the artificial "growth" of acquiring other companies or other company's product lines.

Typically, earnings grow faster than revenue. If a company's top line revenue is growing 10% a year, healthy earnings growth would usually be a bit more, perhaps 12% - 15% a year. These numbers are easy to find if a company's shares are publicly traded, but much more difficult if a company is private. It is well worth researching as much as you can and asking pointed questions during interviews.

Why growth? Because organic organizational growth typically offers advancement opportunities. A company growing revenue and earnings at 10% a year typically needs 5% more employees, more managers, and an occasional Senior VP, if not every year but at least every few years. Most businesses don't scale without needing more humans, even as artificial intelligence promises greater automation. If a company is not growing, people must leave or be fired to open new positions. A company with really strong earnings tends to try new things, offering opportunities for the creative young person to stand out and advance. Companies struggling with earnings all too often try to save and skimp their way to success, taking few risks.

New startups offer the greatest ratio of risk and reward. The upside, if you negotiate well when coming on board, can be huge, but the risk of failure is invariably high, when business models are unproven, the operation is often losing money while trying to build momentum, and the patience of the original investors is running out. The ultimate version of this scenario is to create your own startup, find investors to fund you, and swing for the Bill-Gates-like homerun, but most, understandably, find a job and try to save up some funds so that they have options.

The tide raises all ships. If you have three legitimately attractive offers, look hard at the company that offers the most fertile soil, the one that is growing revenue and earnings consistently, and believes in meritocracy. If you need a tie breaker, consider which company and position will offer greater value on your resume a few years from now. Few people these days stay with a company longer than 5 - 10 years so resume value matters.

Certain job types pay better than others as a job class. Professional selling is such an arena. High-end enterprise software selling tends to be the highest end of the sales profession, and the top companies tend to only hire salespeople already proven at selling software solutions. If you can't manage the leap into a Tier 1 firm right away, there is a good logic in getting hired into a software selling position at a Tier 2 or Tier 3 company, because you are still entering a profession that eventually offers great financial rewards to those with top results.

The bottom line is to land in fertile soil. If you don't get a great landing spot, continue to look even as you start the new job. It makes little sense to spend 5 years of your career launch window in a slot that is not helping you, just because they were "nice enough" to hire you upon graduation.

What about pursuing and earning a master's degree? The answer, if you see your most-likely future within traditional large corporation employment and advancement, is near certainly, yes. There is plenty of evidence that a master's degree is often the tiebreaker that differentiates one candidate for promotion over another. The life-time career earnings with a master's or a PhD degree are invariably better than a bachelor's degree, on average. Whether you pursue your advanced degree on a full-time or part-time basis often will come down to making the best financial decision. See my article at escavg.com/masters for some additional earnings statistics and discussion.

In an upcoming chapter, I will discuss the need to differentiate, and education is a tangible, clear way to position yourself for upper management roles. If you don't find a great "fertile soil" employment option when you graduate with a bachelor's degree, consider pursuing the master's degree right away, which will hopefully add more opportunities for launching in a great way when you graduate.

I made the mistake of hiring on at NCR at a time when revenue growth was non-existent. NCR had a great story that they were poised to surf the wave of open systems, but the results were not showing up in the numbers. Luckily, it wasn't a total waste as I had a great manager in Bruce, and I learned a many valuable lessons from others on the team. But then, I stayed for most of my 20's, hypnotized by five same-role promotions over 7 years, remaining in a company that was unlikely to move a young person into VP slots. If you are wondering what a same-role promo is, a company will have you do essentially the same job — for example, sales — but call you different titles like Associate Account Manager, Account Manager, Senior Account Manager, Executive Account Manager. Each bump gets you a better pay package, but the role essentially remains the same.

In the meantime, a good friend of mine, Phil, perceived NCR's plight more clearly than I did, and looked for more fertile soil, interviewing for better jobs. He moved to Microsoft in the early 90's and progressed quickly through the ranks as Microsoft doubled, and doubled, and doubled again. In 1991, Microsoft had $2B in sales. Today Microsoft is 29 times larger than NCR at over $200B in sales, and Phil became one of the top executives at the company, a clear top 2%'er. The company grew like a weed and Phil, an enthusiastic optimistic guy much like me, rode the wave well. While I'm certain that Phil did it right, but I'm also certain that fertile soil matters a heck of a lot too. In the meantime, NCR has effectively shrunk to ~40% of its former self in currency adjusted for inflation.

The second aspect of launching well is understanding the seasons of your own life. At 22, you might look out on the far-off horizon of your life and think that there is plenty of time. There is not.

Our lives have seasons. School is the first season, and it generally ends abruptly. Your 20's is the brilliant decade, because you will likely never be as brave and tolerant of risk as you are now. Often, your worst-case scenario is having to move back home with your parents for a year while you get your sh*t together, and that is not a terrible option for most recent graduates.

Only a decade away are your 30's, and for many, that means getting serious about starting a family. Wedding rings, a mortgage, dogs, kids, Montessori daycare, all dramatically increase the "what do I have to lose" side of your equation.

Your 40's and early 50's are covered up with great responsibilities, large expenditures, and intense time commitments as kids grow up, challenge parental advice and control, and then spend your savings on college, additional cars, and weddings.

Late 50's and early 60's can bring a new peace if you have stayed healthy. Many people have built unhealthy life habits and are so used to the daily grind that they don't start much new, late in their careers. Then come your late 60's and beyond, a season where some people lose their enthusiasm for struggle and goals, and frankly, everything it means to be young, enthusiastic, and hungry.

While these decades are mere guidelines, the "greater responsibilities" horizon is not far away at all. It lurks at year 30, or 34, but not much later than that. You have less than 520 weeks to take smart risks and launch with authority.

Chapter 5 | Choose your Destiny, Daily

To have any chance of escaping average, there is one personal responsibility that you must accept now, today, if you have not done so already: every choice is your own, and your life's path will be the outcome of your daily choices. You have a choice to go for it, a choice to chart your own course, a choice to persist and see it through, a choice to change directions when you want, a choice to build new, productive habits, a choice to get rid of bad habits, a choice to not overreact to a given situation, a choice to change jobs, or friends, or a mate, a choice to live life however you please. If you stick to the situation that you are in, you are still making a choice, a decision to go with the status quo.

Self-made billionaire, Oprah Winfrey, sums it up this way: *"With every experience, you alone are painting your own canvas, thought by thought, choice by choice."*

The power that you have, when you realize that you can choose to change, is mind-boggling. Imagine that you are a salesperson selling used Fords in a parking lot under a dancing inflatable tall man balloon. For months, your commission bonuses have sucked, as your name seems stuck near the bottom of the leaderboard posted in the break room. What if, one morning as you chew your Einstein's bagel, you decided to act like you were the best sales consultant that Jimmy's Auto Palace had ever seen?

There is a predictable domino effect right after you make any important, life-changing choice.

What if, in the first few weeks, you then studied every competitive car and truck until you knew their data backwards and forward? What if you test drove every applicable car from the competition making notes, what if you read every review, and watched YouTube videos of other reviewers around the world and even created your own videos too? What if you learned everything about financing options, best insurance options, wheel protection policies, and undercarriage coating? What if you showed up to work with an amazing, enthusiastic, positive, can-do attitude, what if you saw yourself as a consultant who wants to genuinely learn about each person who he meets, what if you remembered names, and strived to give them good advice on everything from safety ratings, to recalls, to gas mileage? What if you sent people sincere emails after their visit, returned calls instantly, jotted down their kids' names on your smartphone, and remembered little details about what sports those kids play?

Would the first choice that you made at Einstein's change your financial and career trajectory? What if, a few months later, you made another choice, a choice to interview for a job at the BMW dealership on Main Street since you are atop Jimmy's Auto Palace leaderboard? Or what if you decided to start selling real estate? Or perhaps enterprise software?

Many people stuck near or below average feel somewhat powerless. They believe that they are where they are in life because outside forces have put them there. The top ten percenters, on the other hand, believe that life is 10% what happens to you and 90% how you choose to react to it. If someone cuts you off in traffic, you can, in that millisecond, choose to say *"oh well, no biggie"* or lay on the horn, get angry, and flip the guy off. If you are in a job that is clearly not getting you where you want to be, you can choose to apply for other ones. Every choice at any given moment, is your own.

There is a remarkable gap between the average person's intellectual understanding of the power to choose, and the day-to-day freedom to choose. If you sit down with people over a cup of coffee at Starbucks and chat for an hour, most people will intellectually know and explain that they have the power to choose their path in life. When the setting is right and the pace unhurried, philosophical logic prevails.

Unfortunately, most people don't create time and space to think in their daily life. Most have not developed habits and techniques that would help them find adequate time and space to review and consider things logically.

Instead, many lives are dominated by *"have to"* thinking. I *have to* rush to school because I'm late. I *have to* take a test on Friday, then I *have to* meet my friend at the Galleria to find a dress for the party that I *have to* go to Saturday night, then rush over to the tailor to get it altered. I also *have to* call my mom and beg her for money because I'm going to be short this month, because I *have to* have that dress, and unfortunately, I *have to* pay the rent.

It seems like most people are on the *"have to"* hamster wheel, and don't recognize that they have the power to make far more choices, every step of the way, every day.

You would not *"have to"* rush to school if you made the choice to get up an hour earlier, which is made easier by choosing to go to bed at 10 pm instead of staying up until 1 am. You could have bought that dress months ago when you saw it on a killer 50% off sale, realizing that you would soon need a short black dress for a party during the fall, and had it altered well ahead of time. You could have asked for a little overtime work to pay for the dress, or maybe chosen to eat at home for a few more meals, instead of hoping for your mom's charity.

A person always has the power to choose, even in the blink of an eye. How many times have you had a moment where someone cut you off in traffic? In that split second, you have a choice. Some people — usually the ones that have not learned and habitualized this lesson — will lay on the horn, yell at the person, and drive their own blood pressure through the roof, while impacting their attitude for hours to come, often with additional consequences. There are plenty of stories of people getting shot because they chose road rage. Others on the other hand — the ones who realize that life is 10% what happens to them and 90% how they react to it

— stay zen, say *"oh well, not a problem"* and go on to live another positive day.

We have all seen a few Avengers movies. What if you could pick a superpower for yourself? What would it be? You would probably like a power that could make a great difference in the outcome of your life, and a great difference in the impact that you personally could make while here on Earth.

How would you get your new power? Perhaps you were working late at night on a project in the lab and you were bitten by a radioactive spider that had fallen into a vat of luminescent chemicals. What if, instead of becoming Spiderman, you woke up the next morning with the ability to always make the right decision, the best choice, day in and day out?

Would this power make a big difference in your life? You would take the right job, you would ask the right questions, you would meet the right people, you would find the right spouse, you would invest in the right stock at the right time, you would change jobs at the right moment, you would know when to take a leap of faith on a new start-up. You would decide to sell your venture and change to other investments at the right time too. Your life would indeed change for the better.

Making the right choices makes a huge difference, yet average people are rather random and somewhat careless when they make new choices, or when they choose to stay the course and keep things the same, blindly accepting choices others make for them.

Warren Buffet, one the most successful investors of all time, offered an incredible lesson about making great choices when investing in the stock market when he said: *"I could improve your ultimate financial welfare by giving you a ticket with only 20 slots in it—so that you had 20 punches representing all the investments that you got to make in a lifetime. And once you'd punched through the card, you couldn't make any more investments at all. Under those rules, you'd think really carefully about what you did, and you'd be forced to load up on what you'd really thought about. So you'd do so much better."*

Mr. Buffett's lesson is to make each major decision carefully, thoughtfully, logically.

Here's the wakeup call — while we don't have the power to see the future, we all do have an absolute superpower that most people rarely use — every choice is our own, and creating a framework to thoroughly think through our options is something we can apply every day of our life. Instead of a saying *"F-it, I'm in"*, or *"Heck no, I don't want to try that"*, we can take the time to ask for the advice of mentors and others who have taken a similar path. We can think it through with pen and paper, as decisions look different and are usually clearer, on paper. We have the power to make important choices every day that can change our destiny, our success, our life. Yet most of the time, we choose not to choose for ourselves. How often do people know that they are on the wrong path, they fully know that they are wasting their time, yet they let years and hundreds of opportunities to change go by unexplored.

Yesterday matters less than anyone thinks. Just because yesterday, you were a substandard waiter getting meager tips while doing the minimum to keep the job, it doesn't mean you can't instantly become a great waiter who rakes in better tips today. You can also decide to look for new jobs, to learn a new skill, to get a new degree, to take an online programming class, to change cities. On a personal level, you can choose to forgive, to make up with someone, to become trustworthy starting today, to begin earning trust again. Every choice is your own. With every choice you make, you paint your life. Will you make it a masterpiece or chaotic graffiti?

Choices will matter more in the post-grad universe than they did the first 20-something years of your life, because your academic era of black-and-white, right-or-wrong-answers that the teacher-has-to-grade-fairly is over. You are where you are today because of the choices you have made up to this point, but there were steel guardrails on your road to this point. In five years' time, you will be where you will be, based on the choices that you will make next, and there are no rules, just guidelines. By making better choice after better choice, you would change your trajectory and destiny.

Just because you can, doesn't mean that it will be easy to make the decision and follow through. For example, I have always suffered a fear of heights, but the day I got locked out, I made a choice to embrace my inner James Bond, climb up on a blazing hot roof, walk over the sloped metal five stories above a parking lot, and drop onto the balcony at the other end of the building to get back in. In truth, I realized, halfway across as the smell my smoldering Nikes wafted up to my nose, that this was freaking stupid move, but when you are 22, you don't always think it through. Seven years later, I decided to go skydiving, fear of heights be damned, and had a truly amazing experience because I was "all in" committed. Neither choice was easy to make and neither choice solved my fear of heights, but they proved to me that I can make any choice that I decide to make. Overcoming fears is never easy, no matter if it is heights, public speaking, spiders, betting big on an investment, trying something completely new, or plunging headlong into a new career, but the more you make decisions and try things, the more you realize that you can.

One choice is worth making today. Successful outliers make the contrarian choice to relish change, to embrace change, to seek opportunities. Change is the only constant, yet the average person will tell you that he hates change. I believe there are few things more important than adopting a new phrase — *I love change* — and then start believing and living it.

We all have this make-better-decisions superpower, but most people rarely recognize it or use it on a daily basis. Each free choice has outcomes and consequences. Nobody ever escapes consequences, good or bad. While you can't choose your innate natural abilities, you can make decisions thoughtfully after careful consideration of all the options, you can choose your work ethic, your attitude, your willingness to learn, to embrace change, and to take smart risks.

Chapter 6 | Habits and Designing your Own Operating System

99.9% of us win, lose, add value, earn money, succeed, fail, are happy or sad because of our brain. Our bodies mostly exist to transport us around. If we do manual labor, the body matters a bit, but even so, your noggin is how you add greater value than the average person in the same job. The strongest bricklayer on earth doesn't keep his job if his brain results in lots of workplace injuries. Even the greatest athletes must keep it together mentally when the game hangs in the balance.

There are two kinds of people — those who believe they can choose, decide, and over time, consciously reprogram how they think and what they are, and those who believe that they can't change how they think. There are millions of people who have turned over a new leaf and changed themselves, yet billions make excuses.

If you don't believe that you have the superpower of free choice as discussed in the previous chapter, you might as well make the choice to stop reading the rest of [ESC][AVG], because without that belief, you are hosed. But if you do believe that you can learn and re-program your own operating system, the next step is to understand human nature and how our brain works and conserves energy. Our lives are mostly a product of our habits, combining both our good habits and our bad habits. We are what we do over and over again. Excellence, then, is not an act, not a one-time event, but a habit.

The habits that you choose, adopt, and eventually burn into your own head are the difference between excellence and struggle. This is because it would be exhausting to have to consciously think through every single reaction to every single situation. The same is true if you had to think through "shall I eat", "shall I work out", "shall I take a shower", etc. There is a good reason most people don't keep their New Year's resolution to work out this year —

they never succeed in coding the habit, the routine into their normal life. If you are forced to use conscious thinking and decision-making for the long run, you will find that both mindfulness and willpower wane.

So how does one become excellent and greatly improve his or her odds of the top five percent life? In one sentence, understand the key disciplines of success, coding them into your own mental operating system. The fourth truth or golden rule that I realized over time is that it is up to you to consciously design and ingrain your own habits. Designing your own habits is the key.

This would be easier to do if you didn't already have a mental operating system, if you didn't have other habits, but we all have them. For the last twenty-something years, your coding has been influenced by friends, siblings, parents, enemies, teachers, television, movies, streaming media, advertising, and whatever you found interesting in your environment. Most of it has been subconscious coding, but it is now there. Most people have some bad habits which they choose to keep, dragging them down. It really is easy to stay right where you are today because habits have a powerful grip.

A simple example of changing bad habits is seen when training for a sport like soccer. If you tend to plant your non-kicking foot behind the ball while taking a penalty kick, you will often miss the goal frame as the ball sails too high. Coaches will have you practice and practice, focusing on the plant foot until your head and shoulders are over the ball, not behind it. The result will be keeping the ball low and on frame when the pressure is on during the big game. The process requires practice to get rid of the bad habits while substituting the good habits that produce better outcomes.

In martial arts, practicing forms, perfectly, over and over, ensures that the proper punch, kick, block, and counterpunch are executed during the heat of competition. In basketball, coaches drill home the habits of keeping your shoulders square and your body in balance while shooting a three pointer. In golf, in tennis, in squash, in clay shooting, habitualizing the right mechanics for every moment is crucial. Every sport has optimal mechanics to ensure success and practicing until the optimal mechanics are habitualized is what helps the athlete under the pressure of the moment.

Success on the athletic field and success in life have a lot in common. Step one is to recognize which habits are keeping you from achieving the results you need, while adding new habits and practicing them until they are second nature, so that you can nail it, in the heat of the moment, without thinking. Unfortunately, it is harder to find a skills coach in the game of life than in the game of tennis — without a coach, you often have to be objective, be self-disciplined, and work out habits of success yourself.

Habits have incredible power over your life. Any discipline, any recipe for success, can be followed when using will power and conscious thought but finding the time for conscious thought is hard when the heat is on. Conscious thought is slow and ponderous in relation to what is needed during a difficult moment. As a result, you revert to your habits in the heat of the moment.

In the last few decades, science has shown that habits reside in the basil ganglia section of your brain, not your higher-level conscious-thinking frontal cortex. Work done by the cortex is highly complex, but relatively slow. The cortex requires recalling various bits of memory, comparing the relevance of your memories to the current situation, thinking it through, and deciding what to do, then executing the decision. While this is fine in some environments, such as peacefully studying in a library, it is way too slow if you are a boxer and your opponent just launched a mighty right cross toward your head. It takes about 200 - 250 milliseconds for your vision to transmit the movement to your brain, giving you little time to duck or block the punch. A pro boxer can punch at the astounding speed of 100 milliseconds, so great defensive boxers often anticipate punches before the opponent's movement. There simply is no time for mulling it over.

The same things happen every day in your career. Certain disciplines must become habits for you to succeed. When I first graduated college, I went through six months of professional sales training. The instructors taught many lessons but one that really became a habit for me was to ask *"why do you say that..."* as a response to any unexpected attack by a customer. The key was to buy time to think and understand, instead of arguing and make your predicament worse.

Only months later, and still less than one year from being in training, I walked into a customer's business with a bit of swagger. The Senior VP spotted me and blasted *"Your system sucks!"* across the room in the presence of a large group, obviously stressed over an immediate problem. It was a verbal torpedo designed to destroy the young vendor guy in the navy-blue suit. Without thinking, the months of training kicked in. Instead of turning red, breaking a sweat, stammering, and arguing that our system does not suck, I found myself asking *"Why do you say that?"* in a calm, confident, yet concerned manner. Habits saved me. The SVP launched into a four-minute arm-waving Dennis Miller-like rant, which let me ask more open-ended follow-on questions, gaining lots of information and buying time to think with the prefrontal cortex. By the end of the exchange, I was able to concisely summarize his concerns, and what I was going to do to get to some answers for him in a hurry. Above all else, People want to be understood.

There are thirty or so great disciplines that must be habitualized to improve your odds of escaping average. Beyond deft objection handling, these include things like personal differentiation, freely giving gifts of ideas, resisting negative gossip, and more. I know that you might think that these are conscious prefrontal cortex operations (and they can be), the truth is that you must code your own operating system to react correctly, without having to carefully consider and decide in each situation. For example, a person who must consciously think about "should I tell the truth or not" in any particular instance is unlikely to build a reputation of unquestionable trust and integrity.

The first step is to honestly look in the mirror and evaluate your current situation regarding good habits, bad habits, or no habits. Take a few minutes to take a self-assessment at escavg.com/survey — the survey will be helpful to identify where you will have to focus the most in the future.

Assuming you just now completed the online five-minute survey, you now realize that these questions have been a bit of a preview of the thirty techniques and disciplines of [ESC][AVG]. There are no guarantees, but you will significantly improve your odds of success in life, if you code some of these disciplines into your mind as habits. Just to use one example, if you are clear as to the differentiation that you want to have and want to project consistently to everyone, it becomes second nature to emphasize one, two, or three key differentiating points about yourself whenever you meet others, which leads to becoming more memorable and remarkable in other people's minds.

So how do you take a discipline and make it a habit?

Habits follow a fairly understood cycle. There is invariably a (1) trigger or triggers that (2) cause your habitual mind to go into automatic mode (which saves your brain considerable conscious effort) that then (3) leads to a reward that you find pleasurable or rewarding.

The first step is to recognize what triggers a habitual response.

In a simple example, getting up in the morning triggers a well-established habit of brushing your teeth. Right now, you might go straight from brushing your teeth to making and drinking your first cup of coffee, which rewards your brain with a blast of caffeine.

If you want to add a new habit, it is simple to add your new routine at the end of the established trigger of brushing your teeth. So, let's say you decide that you want to do 10 minutes of stretching as part of an improved health plan. In the first weeks, you might need notes on your toothbrush to start stretching for 10 minutes after the morning brushing session. Only make that coffee after completing the routine. You will find that conscious effort will soon go away — stretching after brushing will simply, magically become the new normal.

It pays to focus. Don't try to add too many new habits at a time, or things become difficult and your odds of success decrease. Once stretching without fail is automatic, you might consider adding "plan my day on paper" for just 15 minutes after that first cup of coffee, before you reward yourself with a second cup or your morning bagel.

Every January, countless people try but fail to add fitness to their day, no matter how well thought out their New Year's resolutions list seemed to be. This happens because they don't focus on the simple mechanics and science of habits. People don't have the will power to keep working out for 365 days. The ones that succeed make it a habit.

Imagine John and Molly both decide on the same resolution: this year, I'm going to join the gym and workout every week.

On January 1st, John decides that he will work out three or four times per week, writing it down on his calendar. Then, every day, he sets an alarm on his smartphone that reminds him at 9 am to work out today. Every day, he must then consciously deliberate if today is the day of the week that he will go to LA Fitness and what he will do when he gets there. When the alarm goes off, John is at work and emails are popping up, he is on a conference call, and some deadline often looms. Bandwidth in his prefrontal cortex is in great demand.

Molly decides to work out every day at 7 am when not on a business trip. She also decides that on odd numbered days, she will do aerobic exercise on the elliptical for 45 minutes, and on even numbered days, she will do a comprehensive weights circuit of machines. As a reward, she decides to always stop and get a small smoothie after the gym. Molly has taken 95% of conscious decision making out of her plan: Molly avoids the conscious decision making and deliberation that John faces of which day to workout, or what workout she will do. Who is more likely to succeed?

Getting rid of bad habits often takes more effort than adding new habits. Step one is taking an honest inventory and writing down triggers that kick off the bad habit. Step two is to find something better to do when that trigger makes you yearn for the old habit, and then step three is to reward yourself in a positive way when you improve on your reaction to the trigger.

Let's say a person has a habit of drinking three or four beers whenever he has a stressful day at work. This is clearly a bad habit that could easily get worse over time. The idea would be to find a better substitute for stress relief than alcohol. Stress is the trigger. Perhaps the right answer could be "any day that I am stressed, I will go to the gym and play basketball" after which I will reward myself with a mini dessert at dinner. Yes, some might say he has changed one bad habit into another, but it illustrates the point that changing bad habits comes down to recognizing triggers, changing the resulting action, and giving your brain a reward for doing it a better way. Keeping a clear paper-based log helps, because the memory plays tricks and seeing one's progress in ink, matters.

Build habits of excellence, consciously, and you are on your way to eclipsing the realms of the average.

Chapter 7 | Finding True North

It is hard to hit a target that you can't see, a target you can't recognize. You must see your target clearly, in your mind's eye.

An important choice to make is writing down your targets for success, your definition of what success means to you. For 99% of people, success targets are not single faceted although near obsession on one target can sometimes bring that one target around more quickly. If all you cared about was becoming the world's greatest juggler while riding a unicycle, and practiced for many hours each day, odds are good that you would become top 1% within a couple of years, and maybe just maybe, hold a Guinness World Record before turning 30, hemorrhoids be damned.

While the unicycle example is a bit stretched, there are people like Alex Honnold who clearly look at success differently than you and I do. If you have never watched it, put *Free Solo* on your list of documentaries to watch. The film is engrossing and entertaining. It will help you understand that defining success and life balance are important topics for an individual to distill. Different things make each of us tick.

For most of us, we have a more balanced view of our success as we come to realize that success and happiness are not the same thing. As we mature, we realize that we have a number of roles in life, which include finding a partner success, family success, social friends success, career success, financial success, fitness success, and more.

When defining what success means to you, consider this question: What makes a person wealthy?

It is never just financial. There are plenty of unhappy people with lots of money. There is nothing wrong with earning, having, and using money, but, when money becomes your exclusive scorecard of self-worth, when money becomes your overriding preoccupation, you become infected by an insidious virus that can ruin your life. Money is only one aspect of true wealth. At its best, excess money is the side-effect benefit of doing something great that solves real problems in the real world.

The "money is all that matters" commercial blitzkrieg brainwashes many people and greatly reduces the optimism that is so vital to long-term success. It is garbage messaging that pollutes the mind. It drives some people into debilitating debt, while others get depressed for the perceived inadequacy of their weekly income, bank accounts, and investment accounts. There are countless stories of super-rich going broke over time as they engage in competitions-of-excess, striving to show off more than another mega-rich frenemy.

There is a lot of truth to the phrase *"you can't take it with you."* No one on their deathbed is checking their investment account balance. We often don't appreciate what we do have. Would you sell your eyes for a million dollars? ...or ten million dollars? Would you sell your son or daughter for that million dollars? Would you forgo good health and accept cancer into your lungs for ten million? It turns out that there is much that we would not sell for millions. These hint at the true aspects of our wealth.

Consider this incomplete list:
- I am wealthy because of my health.
- I am wealthy because of my integrity, and the trust people have in me.
- I am wealthy because of my faith.
- I am wealthy because of my immediate family, and their unconditional love.
- I am wealthy because of my extended family and my role in the bigger group.
- I am wealthy because I have freedom and the ability to make my own choices each day.
- I am wealthy because of my courage.

- I am wealthy because of my relationships with friends.
- I am wealthy because of my mentors.
- I am wealthy because of my personal network of colleagues and associates.
- I am wealthy because of my education.
- I am wealthy because of my reasoning ability, the way I am able to perceive, think, understand, and solve problems.
- I am wealthy because of my emotional IQ that helps me make friends and influence everyone around me.
- I am wealthy because of vitality, my energy to make things happen.
- I am wealthy because of my will power.
- I am wealthy because I believe in learning from setbacks, not treating any event as a failure in itself.
- I am wealthy because of the balance I maintain across the various roles in my life.
- I am wealthy because of my experience, and my life's experiences that have molded my character.
- I am wealthy because of my acute awareness of the world around me and its ramifications.
- I am wealthy because of my unusual wisdom for my age.
- I am wealthy because of my ability to learn and grow in understanding every day of my life.
- I am wealthy because I live in a time of extraordinary opportunity in an extraordinary place. People had few choices just a few centuries ago as they farmed for their own dinner.
- I am wealthy because of my optimism, by hopes, my dreams, my goals, my reasons for living.
- Oh yes, lest I forget, I am wealthy because of my bank accounts and investment accounts.

Two dozen aspects of wealth, admittedly incomplete. Clearly, there is more to wealth and your net worth than just the financial account. Note that wealth, in any category, must be age-adjusted. If you compare your assets in the 'network of colleagues' category when you are 24 to someone who is 48, chances are that the person who has lived and worked six times longer as an adult than you will have many more colleagues and a broader network than you.

It's a heck of a lot easier to define what success means to you if you can figure out your one True North, the one overriding purpose to your life.

True north is not like individual goals, although it is best if your goals all point to your true north. Right about now, I suspect you are thinking *"Whoa, I just graduated college and you want me to come up with my grand overall purpose on Earth? Are you fricken kidding me?"* I totally get it, I understand that you might not be able to figure it out right now, but I simply want you to keep the importance of figuring it out in mind. Some people — a lot of people — never figure it out, and they are worse off for their own failure. The sooner that you do figure your single most important purpose out, the likelier you are in achieving it and escape average.

Wise people have put it this way — what's the twenty words that you would like to see on your tombstone when you have moved on from this life? Then, what are the three sub-bullets that you would like to be the basis of the eulogy that someone eloquently shares during your funeral?

That's personal true north and it usually fits on just one PowerPoint slide: what do you want your 40, 50, maybe 60 'productive adult' years to add up to when you are done? Pre-college years don't often count as you are simply pouring your mental foundation and most people have later years in life when they simply coast at the end. What future would make you proud?

"Why am I here on Earth?" is a tough question. There are many valid purposes - but you must choose what feels most harmonious with your inner self. An example of an excellent purpose can be as simple as "I want to help people heal when they are sick." Another is that I want to help people defend themselves in the court of law. Or perhaps, I want to raise an extraordinary family that learns the best of values. Perhaps you were put on earth to invent solutions to big problems that plague society. What would make you proud of yourself, other people's opinion aside?

From these examples, I hope it is clear that your purpose is not the same as your vision. Purpose is a grand statement of what you want to accomplish in general. Vision deals with "envisioning" your future - your position in your life many years into the future, in far more specific terms. Using one of my examples above, the person who decided their purpose was to "help heal people who are sick" would evaluate and decide between a wide variety of visions of their future - one person might decide to become a surgeon, another a medicine researcher, a third might become a physical therapist, a fourth might have the vision of building clinics, and a fifth might become an author, writing books about preventive medicine or even health-oriented cookbooks. All these are valid visions that are in balance with this person's core purpose.

How do you start defining your true north? I would suggest brainstorming (on paper or a dry erase whiteboard) and write down your personal principles that you want to live by, your own personal commandments that you never want to violate. Narrow these down, distill them to your personal top 10.

Over thousands of years, one theme has been tested true: any purpose that is completely self-centered is personally destructive. This wisdom is taught in every religious tradition because it is universal. Imagine if someone defined his true purpose as becoming financially rich, rich, rich. He may, in fact, become rich, but such a purpose will naturally steer him out of balance with his surrounding world, and steer him inevitably, inexorably toward greed and jealousy, corrupting his integrity. Think Bernie Madoff, although there are hundreds of thousands who are far lower profile than Bernie. There is no peace and happiness to be found when one focuses exclusively on himself. Unfortunately, this is not the message we see most often from Hollywood, from the media, or from the advertising gurus on Madison Avenue where self-centered ego maniacs are often held up as heroes. This barrage of messages is flat-out wrong.

Daydream your best case ten years from now, 10, 20, 30, 40 years from now — in writing. Compare that to your written principles. Figuring out what you really want, what's the one thing that will make you proud of what you have accomplished, matters. It is not easy, and you will want to revisit this every year. You will find that you will pivot and change over time, but you want to make sure you are headed in the right direction for you.

For a few people, their purpose just comes to them, easily, and with great clarity. These people are truly blessed. A young adult who just knows, really knows, that she wants to be a medical doctor is off to the races. She is truly fortunate, because when a person has a clear picture in her mind, it is amazing how week after week, month after month, year after year, all activities add up to the achievement of her vision. She is willing to do the work and make the sacrifices. For others, discovering their purpose takes some time. Most people go throughout their lives lost - they never figure out the core of what they want to be. It is not surprising that these people remain clustered around the average. You must find and write down your purpose as soon as you can. Yes, purpose can change a bit over time - after all, we all become wiser about knowing ourselves and the realities, good and bad of the world we live in as we build up experience. But a defined purpose is our guiding light.

Purpose in fact, gives concrete meaning to life. Once you find the one thing you were born to do, or the one thing you were born to be, the reason you are breathing, all life's decisions fall into place. Everything becomes so much simpler. You just know. Purpose gives you "why" and "why" fuels you through tough times and hard work.

Define your true north. Let your imagination run. If it is in you, make your purpose grand. Make it extraordinary. If you do, the results, thirty or forty years hence, will surprise even you.

Put all this work in writing, in your permajournal system so that it never gets lost. As a reminder, my thoughts about permajournalling are found at escavg.com/permanotes.

Chances are you don't have true north etched in stone yet. That's ok. It still matters to start bringing success into focus. Grab your pen and, without thinking for days, jot down what does extraordinary success mean to you if you look three years into the future? What's your best case career-wise success three years from today? Same question, but health-wise? What has improved in the next three years? Same question, but in your personal, social life. What do you imagine? What do you see for your relationship with your family? Same question again, but this time in terms of self-improvement — how are you better, personal capability-wise, three years from today? One more time, how do you imagine your financial situation three years from now.

Graduating college, these "roles" are the minimum to consider, but of course, there are more or will be more in the future. You must find your own true north over time, while understanding what is important to you right now. Don't subdivide your attention and multitask. You will not succeed in starting your new business venture while squandering your money and health away, drinking in clubs until 2 am, four or five nights each week. Progress doesn't happen that way.

Take a second to scribble three bullets on each of the roles below. What is success defined as to you (at a minimum), three years from today:

Career-wise:	• • •
Health-and-fitness-wise:	• • •
Social-life-wise:	• • •
Family-relationship-wise:	• • •
Self-improvement-wise:	• • •
Financial-investment-wise:	• • •
Mentor-wise:	• • •

Any person sitting on the launch pad needs to target finding and building a network of mentors. Sage advice is important when the world conspires to distract you and spend your time on others' behalf. Getting five excellent, diverse, carefully considered, and well-intentioned opinions, when facing any tough decision, will help you make wise decisions beyond your years, wasting less of your precious time. Remember that great, thoughtful decision-making is a most-important superpower that must be developed.

Once you have defined your targets three-years out, repeat the exercise but now make it 7 - 10 years into the future. Yes, this gets fuzzy as it is hard to see over the horizon, but it is well worth doing. You will not hit a target if you are not aiming for it.

It is important to realize that decisive, massively committed action beats thinking alone, 100% of the time. Once you know what success looks like to you, create plans on paper. At a minimum, an action plan includes breaking each target goal into milestones, and then putting those milestones on paper and on a calendar. Break milestones into monthly accomplishment 'mega-tasks' so that you see and feel your progress. Momentum is easy to lose so creating and executing a plan that has tangible progress weekly is best.

After you have a plan, don't overthink it. Be decisive, be committed, and start taking massive action. Action drives learning, action drives adjusting, action conquers many of the hurdles in front of you. Lack of decisive, committed action is why so many truly talented, super smart people do not escape average. When in doubt, get out of your comfort zone, take action, and learn from setbacks.

Lastly, review what success means to you at least twice per year. Consider setting alerts to review and revise your plans every July 4th weekend and every New Year's weekend. These weekends are perfect "triggers" to keep your targets in focus for the next six months.

Chapter 8 | Opportunities are Often Disguised as Hard Work

The average person does not want to work all that hard. A simple truth to remember is that if an opportunity was easy and straightforward to accomplish, someone else would have already done it. This is why there will always be great new opportunities waiting for someone to take decisive committed action and do the hard work.

We absolutely, positively live in a world of abundance, a world that is steadily getting better, full of new opportunities. Unfortunately, evolution over thousands of years has pre-wired our brains to notice and pay more attention to danger more than progress. This made great sense when the most successful humans were the ones who avoided the lions, but much of the news media and social networking world today thrives by feeding the appetite for fear, uncertainty, and doubt. Just read the click-bait headlines. In virtually every way, change is for the good, yet most average people choose and adopt a scarcity and fear mentality.

The greatest disservice the media does to society is to focus on the negative versus the positive. The old newspaper slogan "If it bleeds, it leads" is as prevalent today as it was fifty years ago. People play their part — they keep clicking and watching the horror and outrage of it all. I was in London on the day that Brexit passed. If you watched through CNN's little window, there were mass protests and celebrations throughout the UK. On the ground in London, a city of nearly nine million, there were a couple of hundred people, maybe a thousand at the peak, in one square holding up some signs and flags for an hour or two. The cameras had their story.

The truth is that progress continues to accelerate. Opportunities are multiplying like rabbits. A wise person who looks past the news and people's social media chatter and sees reality, a person who decides to become a life-long student, a person who embraces change, a person who looks for and seeks opportunities, will find an endless supply.

If you don't believe, answer just three questions using a piece of paper and some bullet points: How will robotics change my life in the next 20 years? How will 3D printing change my life in the same time frame? How will advances in artificial intelligence make things better too? There are a lot of obvious opportunities for improvement, and these are only three areas of many.

Although you will find an endless supply of opportunities, nothing will be as easy as you think it will be. Rarely will a project take less time than you thought. If you want to escape average and become a top success, you will have to work harder and smarter than average. There is no substitute for effort while others slouched are on their couch bingeing Netflix shows.

People who take massive, committed, focused, gritty action are those who will make progress, make mistakes, learn from their mistakes, adapt, overcome, and succeed. Southwest Airlines' famous founder, Herb Kelleher, had a great quote well worth remembering: *"We have a strategic plan — it's called doing things."* Prolific, best-selling author of 86 books and a net worth of $500M, Stephen King, put it this way: *"Talent is cheaper than table salt. What separates the talented individual from the successful one is a lot of hard work."*

I witnessed people self-justifying their average level of effort at every stop of my career. You will too as it's not hard to spot it. There is an overriding flaw in a lot of people's thinking: It is the feeling of entitlement. Many people feel they 'deserve' success and the benefits of success for one reason or another and not their contribution in the present time. No matter if you graduated with honors from the Ivy League or if you graduated from Central High School, no one is going to hand you a bucket of gold and thank you for what you did in the past. The real-world universe doesn't care about yesterday, or last month, or last year.

Hustle matters. One important lesson I learned from my first team leader, Sam, was to respond to requests as fast as possible. People appreciate it, they learn that you care, they see that you hustle, and it's actually not much harder than procrastinating and then responding later. Actions speak louder than words and Sam's formula showed every customer and every colleague that he could be counted on. A lot of people might use excuses for why they can't respond quickly but then you find the story that Sam Walton, one of the richest entrepreneurs on earth, replied to every voice mail on the same day. Yes, the discipline might make you a little late for happy hours at the pub, but you will be better off for it.

When in doubt, take decisive action. Planning is important, but only when it leads to committed action that gets you all the way to the finish line. No athlete wins an Olympic medal for wishing he or she would qualify — athletes must practice until they bleed, until they have given their all. No one wins an Olympic medal for starting the race — he or she must take the action needed to finish strong.

Thomas Edison observed: *"Genius is one percent inspiration and ninety-nine percent perspiration. Great accomplishments depend not so much on ingenuity as on hard work."*

Don't get hung up on a project looking hard to do. *"Gee, robotics looks hard."* That is exactly why there is opportunity! If the potential of robotics fires you up, jump in and start experimenting, start making some mistakes, and start making some progress. Don't be like all the average people who say *"robotics looks hard, I don't know much about it, so I'll avoid it."*

The successful outliers, the ones who escape average, embrace hard work and learning. They are not afraid of the work. They love the discipline of it, the trade-offs they are making to win. A lot of average people, on the other hand, see hard work as punishment. That's a key difference, and the difference is in your mind.

One of the main reasons I got a great start on real-life was that I came from a family that valued hard work. I then got lucky and was hired by a manager who encouraged hard work, and I was mentored by Sam, who was a great example of hard work, committed decisive action, and whatever-it-takes mentality. By the time I was 25, I was laser focused on making things happen, even if I had to burn the midnight oil for weeks or months. I discovered that you will always find plenty of opportunities if you look for them and you don't change your mind when it takes more work than expected.

Suggested books: Read *Factfulness* by Hans Rosling, Anna Rosling Ronnlund, Ola Rosling to better understand how quickly the world is getting better. It is well worth the read as is *Grit* by Angela Duckworth.

Chapter 9 | Leverage the Greatest Technology — Pale Ink

Imagine hoping to win the Superbowl without a playbook your team has learned, practiced, and will execute with precision.

Imagine building the house that you live in without an architect first creating blueprints that can be shared across all the subcontractors.

Imagine leading a SWAT team, invading a bank where the bad guys are holding hostages at gunpoint, without looking at the building plans to see how the rooms and entries are positioned, then briefing the team members on what they will do.

It is hard to imagine success in any of these attempts without clear, specific, detailed plans and contingency plans, isn't it?

Thinking on paper, planning on paper, making notes on paper — whether old-school ink or new-school digital ink — is crucial to success. Even the palest of ink is better than the best memory. Studies have proved that handwritten notes are more effective than typing on a keyboard.

Early on in my sales career, I felt my mind was an awesome steel trap. It seemed like I effortlessly remembered everything that each customer said to me, and I was able to leverage those details to build strong connections and relationships. Before long, I was transferred to San Antonio and focused on other clients. Trusting my mind seemed fine, until one day, only a year later, I was drafted to help on my old account in the Carolinas. I suddenly realized that 75% of the detail had evaporated just that quickly. I could not remember the names of my contact's spouses or kids, I could not remember what teams and sports each customer cheered for, I didn't remember their alma maters (as this was before LinkedIn) — many of the details that mattered to having a better than average relationship had disappeared, seemingly replaced by the details of new customers I had met in San Antonio.

There's a lot of truth to the phrase: out of sight, out of mind. Yet in the real-world, having an ever-growing personal network is an asset that builds in value over the years, if you can keep the details fresh and reconnect every so often. Luckily, I learned this vaporization problem while still in my twenties. I started keeping written, organized notes and those notes have easily quadrupled the network I would have built without them.

Along the way, I found that simply using ink and paper more often helped me plan better. I made plans for the year, and for each account. Seeing each plan in ink helped resolve inconsistencies and prioritize projects logically.

What journals do the top successful people use? At a minimum, please consider:

1. An idea journal — a place to jot down all those wonderful random thoughts that you have when a flash of genius strikes you. But it should be more than just certified genius thoughts. It must contain little clues, little ideas than someday might become more. Never make the mistake of collecting these ideas in your daily journal alone. Every good idea must migrate to the idea journal so that it isn't lost in the future.

2. A project journal – a small planning-and-progress journal for each important project that you decide to take on. If a project is truly important to your future, do not simply mix your thinking and tasks and milestones into your normal daily bullsh*t task management system, or you will likely lose sight of important steps in the middle of all the other urgent but less important busy work.

3. A daily highlights journal — a place to jot down highlights of the day. If you spot an idea in this journal that is worthy, highlight it, then copy it to your idea journal as soon as you can. Ideas make the world go around.

4. A goals journal — a place to jot down ideas for the future that may later turn into plans and eventually steady project (at which time they will need their own planning journal)

5. A calendar — this will most likely be electronic on your smartphone for the convenience of always having it with you. I suggest having a personal calendar that shows all important events including work ones. Why? Because the day you change companies, your work calendar will disappear and with it, the reminder log of meetings and contacts that you made.

6. Chronological detailed notes — even scant notes will help you remember conversations and events.

7. People contact notes — make notes about people while you talk to them. This is best transferred to an electronic system to allow you to search for your notes by person quickly, later when you will meet them again.

8. Self-improvement log — It is easy to miss focusing on self-improvement. By logging anything you have done in this regard, it will help you achieve a balance between daily work and improvement that will matter in the longer run.

One final step helps. While longhand notes are best for remembering and thinking, storing them in digital format is best for long-term availability, safety, and ease of finding them again. On the last day of each month, review and scan your notes to an electronic format, then send the copy to your electronic archive.

Technology changes quickly. I have a recommended technology brief / blog post with recommendations online, so that it can be updated after this book is published. See escavg.com/journals for greater detail on journaling and keeping your journals safe.

Chapter 10 | First Downs and Your Number One Priority

While all these disciplines matter, this one stands out as one of the most important habits that you must learn. There's a heck of a lot of wishful thinking and idle talk in the real-world. People look to impress others by what they plan to do. Self-initiative and action-speaks-louder-than-words professionals are few and far between.

Above average people do one thing that is different than average people: they clearly identify their one top priority right now, they remember what their top priority is on a daily basis, and they make measurable progress on that #1 priority every week until it is accomplished. These achievers take decisive action. They learned the childhood lesson from Aesop's Tortoise and the Hare fairy tale: steady progress wins the race.

The average person will tell you that he has a half dozen "top priorities" — which means that he is scattered in his focus, dividing his will power fuel. A wise man once said, *"If you chase two rabbits, both will escape."* The truth of our 'modern' lives is if you chase six priorities, all six will elude you. The word priority was never a plural until recently, for good reason.

Time and time again, I have watched sales professionals struggle when they were given too many prospect companies to call on in their assigned patch. It's hard to do a great job on any one of them when pulled in every direction. At one time, I had the opportunity to sell to every account west of the Mississippi River, after I joined an IBM value-added reseller headquartered in the Southeast. When faced with so much territory, and a bonus plan that rewarded one's total volume of business, I quickly learned that success could be best found by winning one big account at a time, before moving on to the next. In just five years, my patch grew from $1M / year into a $30M / year sustainable business because I focused our efforts on large accounts that would produce consistent year-over-year revenue. Chase one rabbit at a time.

Top-tier successful people make a strategic goal their priority. What do I mean by strategic? It means that your goal, your project, your mission, whatever it is, will have lasting value three months from now, and it will probably still have value three years from now. Strategic projects have value in the longer term while busy work only matters in the next few days or weeks. 'Will this mission matter next year' is a great acid-test to use to decide if something deserves to be your top priority.

It sounds simple, but it is not easy. Often, things that matter long-term represent hard work with little short-term benefit. People look at the next step on their #1 priority, shudder a bit because it looks like an ugly frog to swallow, and then decide to work on the other, easier items on their list. To be a top-tier success, you must take on the next item next, each day without fail, no matter if it is easy or hard, while you still have will power, maximum positivity, and energy. Do not skip over your strategic priority to work on something easier or someone else's 'urgent yet less important' task that was assigned to you.

Make no mistake: the most strategic, valuable things to do are usually the ones that no one is asking you to do, the ones that usually have no deadline. They are the missions that are important but not urgent. For this reason, most people work on urgent tasks, tasks that others are asking for, while procrastinating on the items that could lead them to greatness. Good things to do get in the way of great things to do, all the time.

Like every aspect of [ESC][AVG], you must focus on "making strategic first downs" a good habit. Until it is a habit, until it is triggered daily without fail, until you take massive, committed action, you will be unlikely to become a top achiever.

By doing your big rock task first, there will be time for all the smaller tasks, the small rocks that you feel you must do as well. Most average people, during their all-too-average day, do the small tasks first, only to find that there is no time, will power, and energy left for the big task that is strategic and matters in the long run. Watch this short YouTube video right now to better understand this big-rock concept: escavg.com/bigrocks

The more specific your plan is, the easier this becomes. Let's say that your #1 strategic goal is to land a job at XYZ Company, because you are sure that that company is fertile ground for your career, growing revenues at a stellar 25% per year. This goal comes into better focus when you decide that you want an account executive position, and even better, when you decide that you want that AE position in their Finance Software division. You then search on XYZ's website for open positions, you watch YouTube videos to familiarize yourself with the product lines and the competition, you figure out the hiring managers via LinkedIn and try to connect with other people you might be working with, you ask people to meet you at Starbucks to get their advice, you apply on XYZ's recruiting portal, and you fine-tune your resume to appear a great fit for that specific job description. Each one of these next steps becomes part of your plan for success, and each next step is instantly actionable, without lots of time lost to reconsidering what to do next.

Pale ink is greater than the best of memories. I suggest creating a special extra calendar in Google Calendars or Outlook Calendars to track your selected Strategic Big Rock for the week and the day.

No matter how massive, how daunting a challenge is, you can and will solve it one step at a time. Focus on today's specific mission. When you stare at the enormity of what you are taking on, it becomes too easy to throw your hands up and surrender. Those who take progress one day at a time succeed.

Finally, as you make your plans for your top priority, I suggest outlining not only your best-case plan "A", but put a few hours of thought into contingency plans — your Plan B and Plan C. Why? Because one of the secret keys to success is learning to adapt and overcome. If you always know what your priority is, and you have multiple plans to get to the finish line, you are far more likely to not quit after trying just one tactic, but rather, to adapt, to succeed.

Speed often kills. It matters less as to how fast you are going, but going in the right direction is of utmost importance. Make a strategic first down, or two, every week without fail.

Chapter 11 | Taming the Dragon

In the last chapter, we explored a crucial idea: Many of the most successful people focus and make progress, a first down, on their #1 top priority goal every week. There is an underlying dragon hiding in the back of our minds that tries to sabotage this all-important life habit: Everyone struggles with procrastination. If a person learns the right disciplines and builds the habits to overcome procrastination, his or her chances of escaping average skyrocket. Understanding this dragon and how it is becoming stronger in our tech-fueled world is important to keeping it on a leash.

We love our smartphones. They have given us the power to do so much, to stay connected to others wherever we are, to take pictures, to get dates, to buy tickets and make reservations at any given moment. But there are two sides to every coin. The apps on the ever-present smartphone have taught us to become hopelessly distracted, as though we have attention deficit disorder even though biologically 90%+ do not. Texts, Snapchats, Instagram, TikTok, Facebook, email alerts, breaking news alerts, and every other pop-up from millions of apps, train us to stop what we are doing and turn our attention back to the app-of-this-minute. We have been trained by Silicon Valley's developers and AI algorithms to learn a bad habit that resembles ADD. Once we have willingly allowed ourselves to be reprogrammed by our electronic collar, we continue to flutter our attention from one thing to another, even during the rare moments when the smartphone is out of the room. Just try writing a paper on your PC or Mac and count how many times you jump around to look at something in a different browser tab in just 30 minutes.

Changing an existing habit is much harder than adding a good new habit, but it can be done.

The great news is that you now recognize the pattern, and you have all the tools that you need to build a habit of getting stuff done, especially the stuff that is of strategic importance. I struggled with procrastination for decades of my life. My procrastination dragon is always lurking and can strike at any time, stealing a day, or a week, or even a month away if I let down my guard.

The cold hard truth is no one is great at multitasking. The people who say that they are great at it are also the people who are most likely to stress themselves out, doing less than their best on everything in their lives. Even computers don't multitask but rather quickly switch between multiple things, doing one task at a time. The difference is that a computer "knows" exactly the next step when it efficiently switches back and forth while the human mind takes a much more ponderous path to get focused on the next. Even when you are not falling prey to multitasking, 'good' things to do are often the very things that get in the way of 'great' things to do. Great things to do are the ones that are supporting your strategic priority, the one goal that you have decided to accomplish which will yield long term value. Often, accomplishing greatness takes getting into a state of flow, when your mind gives the task at hand 100% commitment and you completely lose track of time.

Step one is to take a hard look and turn off every superfluous notification that you can. Getting notified of every email and social post torpedoes your focus. I set up a second "high priority" email box that no one knows I have. I then create filters in my main email account to forward emails I want notifications for to that extra email box. This proactive filtering puts me in charge of what matters to me. That second box is the only one that sends me a notification. Unfortunately, text messages are harder to prioritize but putting some percentage of conversations on silent / do not disturb is an idea worth considering.

After you have reduced the bings and the buzzes, the habit that you need to beat procrastination and distraction is to reserve a time slot where you put the rest of the world aside, an hour where you don't multitask. Start small with 30 minutes a day, then work your way up to 60 minutes and then 90 minutes per day. The 90 minutes might be three independent 30 minute sessions on three different strategic tasks but that's perfectly fine. The key is to only focus on the one important thing that you have planned and decided to do during that time slot.

Reward yourself after your zen timeslot. I personally write it down as a "great time invested" note on my calendar, so that I can see the steps I've taken toward one of my top goals and then I refill my cup of coffee. Remember Aristotle's golden rule: "We are what we repeatedly do. Excellence, then, is not an act, but a habit."

By leaving my smartphone in another room and by working in one full screen window, I have found that my 30 minutes of commitment sometimes magically transforms into 60 or 90 minutes of focused "flow" time. This doesn't happen every day and it is not always easy, but you get better at it over time. If you are writing a book, you often struggle and write something that is obviously substandard but, if you refuse to open a new tab and look at random stuff on Amazon or Facebook, you are slowly but surely building the muscle memory to retake control of your life.

Procrastination is the gravity that keeps most people down. You can adapt and overcome because procrastination is a bad habit, not a genetic aspect of your DNA. Our minds are reprogrammable. Start by figuring out your top goals and priorities. Make specific plans, distilled down to specific next steps, so that you have decided what exactly needs to be done. Train yourself to stick to the important task for an uninterrupted 30 minutes and you are well on your way. Write your successes down and be grateful when you overcome distraction temptations. Building great habits takes effort and patience.

If I could beat the procrastination dragon, you can too, because my dragon had a death grip on me years ago. To defeat it, I raised the stakes: I decided to not look at my work email in the morning until I finished my first 30 minute "focused" time block, no matter how late in the morning that was. That was a heck of a motivator, since I could easily miss a conference call or meeting by not checking email. To avoid the ugly risk of missing meetings, I forced myself to focus and make progress during the 6:30 - 7:00 am slot, hot coffee in hand. It was an interesting way to start each day, but I now can "disappear from the urgent world" for an hour or two, with a well-established 'focus' habit that I know helps me succeed.

If my suggestions don't get you over the top with procrastination, Tim Urban, the smart, funny, and fresh creator of the WaitButWhy.com blog, writes about the evils of procrastination, the concepts of never wasting a week because life is shorter than you think, and working on the strategic, important stuff as much as possible. I recommend checking out four web links I have curated here (escavg.com/tim), one of which is his brilliant and witty TED talk. Tim created a weekly life calendar which inspired me to create a tracking spreadsheet for the most important accomplishment of each week for the rest of my life. If you want a free copy for your own use, visit escavg.com/freebee.

Chapter 12 | Consciously Differentiate

Most success is success within a society or group. Humans are social.

Like it or not, it is important to be noticed, to be memorable. People who are invisible don't get promoted for years if ever, people who blend in have fewer friends and associates in their network, people who appear average usually remain average.

Step one is just becoming memorable. Are you memorable already? If not, how do you become memorable in a positive light? The easiest way is to have a differentiated appearance, but appearance is but one step. It usually doesn't change your destiny, but it is still better — far better — than blending in. No one likes the fact that people judge the book by its cover, but people invariably do judge within seconds of meeting you, mostly based on visual clues. When in doubt, dress 10 - 20% better than others at the same event. It can't hurt unless you try too hard and no longer look authentic and appropriate.

Studies have found that people with alliteration in their names tend to succeed more often in life. Why? Because their names are easier to remember. Other studies have shown that taller than average people get promoted more often. Why? They are easier to notice and remember as well.

You can't WOW someone without clear and obvious differentiation. Be mindful and have a plan. You must differentiate, in an obvious enough way so that people, most of whom are always thinking about themselves, notice, while staying connected to your own realm of authenticity. It is hard to fake it until you make it, when you are faking something that is not genuinely you, inside.

Remember that in the real-world, there are no black and white answers. Differentiation is crucial when few results and measures are truly objective. It was easier in college when they graded your exams.

Madonna was one of the most vivid examples of success through differentiation in the 80's and is now, quite easily, one of the richest pop music artists of all time, worth some $800M. She managed to burst onto the scene by carefully riding the edge of sexual and religious controversy. To give her credit, her ability to sing and dance improved dramatically with her commercial success, and that doesn't happen without coaching, hard work, and determination. Madonna is smart and has figured out how to stay fresh and relevant across forty years when few pop artists do, but her overall marketing hype, and her marketing refreshes, were fueled by differentiation and people talking about that differentiation. In a lot of ways, Lady Gaga followed Madonna's shock-people-into-noticing-you formula a few decades later. I wonder if Madonna herself drew some inspiration from a young Elton John.

In the real-world, you must differentiate, but being controversial like Madonna or Lady Gaga in a Fortune 500 setting will result in a quick exit, so finding the right way to be different, but still appropriate, is an art.

Here's the good news — there is plenty of opportunity to succeed because few people consciously differentiate themselves, especially at 22 or 24. Some people start figuring out the importance by 30, but many never do, or are simply afraid to take what they perceive as a risk. The truth is that not consciously differentiating yourself is the bigger risk.

Start by asking yourself what makes you unique? Decide what first impressions you want to make when meeting others, items that not only make you unique but are also authentic to your true character? Don't forget to write it down. Then, ask yourself what you can do differently to make these aspects a bit clearer and more obvious. Assume that most people don't listen well — because they are often thinking about themselves and preparing what they will say next.

If you are coming up empty for ideas right now, here are a few suggestions. Unfailingly "Do what you said you would do" is a brilliant starting point, because few live this way. Unfailing honesty is also a brilliant adoption because the majority fudge the facts. Honesty leads to trust. Another idea is to be a super-listener, always asking follow-up questions and remembering what other people say, on the way to discovering what makes each person special. Smiling a lot, laughing a lot is not only a great way to be more memorable, but you will find that people are naturally attracted to a person who they see as positive and uplifting.

A great trick is to always Google or search on LinkedIn before you meet someone. Just finding out a few facts will help you. Then, think through the impression that you want to make. For example, if you want to come across as confident, think about projecting confidence right before you walk into the Starbucks to meet. You will be amazed as to how simple five-minute visualization helps you project the impression you want, and helps you become more memorable.

In the last few years, I discovered that it is incredibly easy to differentiate yourself and get noticed leveraging social media, even if you work in an exceptionally large company. Few people create blog posts, podcasts, and videos, yet this is exactly what the hyper-connected world is clamoring for. I started using videoscribe.co software to develop "explainer" videos like this one: escavg.com/whiteboard — and it instantly brought me notoriety within my company. Since, I've expanded to presentations on YouTube and my own free-standing blog site. Any young professional can leverage YouTube, LinkedIn, Instagram and the rest to create an on-line presence that shows off their passion and knowledge, while establishing their differentiation.

Finally, don't ignore education, not just for the learning but for the differentiation factor. If you want to rise in your profession, having an advanced degree is often a great tiebreaker when executives are looking to promote someone into management. If you look at the resumes of the Senior VP's and Executive VP's at most companies, the majority all have the education stamp-of-approval that comes with an MBA or other advanced degrees.

Chapter 13 | Unstoppable Force of Nature

Most people are their most enthusiastic before the high school years start. High school then changes things dramatically. It becomes more cool to be cool, not to stand out, not to risk appearing too enthusiastic. Yet unquenchable enthusiasm for life, for your job, for your hobbies, for your pursuits is exactly what makes things happen.

No one wins a medal at the Olympics without belief and optimism. Optimism is the only religion that makes sense if you want to escape the fat part of the bell curve and become a top achiever. Realism doesn't get it done because realists by definition settle for the status quo, while pessimists spend most of their time telling themselves and others that a plan will never work. Stop saying phrases like 'it is what it is' or 'such is life' because this pervasive realist mantra will hurt your chances.

In 2010, I found myself running low on optimism. I had started my own smartphone software company about five years earlier, we had grown quickly on the BlackBerry device and then got torpedoed by the rapid rise of the iPhone. Although we tried to pivot to the Apple platform, the Cocoa / Objective-C developers who came from the Mac world had a distinct advantage versus us Java guys, and the design of the early Apple AppStore didn't mesh with our higher-end, high-value, premium-priced products. By the time we figured it out, landing near the top pages of our categories in the App Store was mission impossible.

After struggling with finding my optimism, I found the solution by creating a personal blog at optimisman.com, which I invite you to visit. Writing is a great way to reflect on the way you are thinking, and, over time, reprogram your own perspective and mental operating system. Within a year, I was once again seeing unlimited opportunities and finding the silver linings in the dark clouds of problems, challenges, and crises. The longer I wrote, the brighter my own inner spark glowed. By 2012, I was back to full power.

I learned that you can't take events out of your control too personally. The same planets that aligned for Apple's greatest hit were the ones that nuked BlackBerry and took us out with it. I also discovered that you must learn how to not give a rat's ass about what most other people think, while you pursue your own dreams and agenda. It is not enough to just say this without conviction — you must really not give a sh*t. Ignore the critics.

This quote from President Teddy Roosevelt is dead on right: "It is not the critic who counts; not the man who points out how the strong man stumbles, or where the doer of deeds could have done them better. The credit belongs to the man who is actually in the arena, whose face is marred by dust and sweat and blood; who strives valiantly; who errs, who comes short again and again, because there is no effort without error and shortcoming; but who does actually strive to do the deeds; who knows great enthusiasms, the great devotions; who spends himself in a worthy cause; who at the best knows in the end the triumph of high achievement, and who at the worst, if he fails, at least fails while daring greatly, so that his place shall never be with those cold and timid souls who neither know victory nor defeat."

Winston Churchill summed it up concisely:
> *"Success consists of going from failure to failure without loss of enthusiasm."*

In the previous chapter, we discussed the need to effectively differentiate yourself. You must pick your differentiators and then make sure that others see them clearly. Enthusiasm can absolutely be a great differentiator. In this day and age, how well you work within a team matters and positive energy can infect your group and help it reach new heights. Just don't be weirdly giddy about it — genuine enthusiasm is marked by being a true believer who cares a lot, not by someone acting like a eighth-grade cheerleader at a junior high football game, cheering to score a touchdown when her team is on defense and backed up to their goal line.

Here is a simple, practical hack to help you: practice doing 10 - 15% more than expected on every project that you decide to take on. Once you have this habit, you will be amazed at how often people notice your effort and attitude.

Everyone runs low on energy and belief occasionally. Don't be surprised that you will too someday. Gratitude is a magical re-charger and the most important key to daily happiness. Without it, realistic optimism and passion fade during tough times. As I'm a committed ink-matters person, I would suggest writing at least one thing that you are grateful for in your chronological journal daily. Review these, especially when feeling a little low. I've also found that one of the best ways to stoke your flames is to help others. Go help people who will never pay you back and you will discover the fountain of eternal optimism.

Stay passionate and you will go far.

Chapter 14 | Creative Idea Hero

Fresh ideas matter. They always have and always will. Ideas have sparked revolutions. Ideas have transformed people's lives. Ideas have founded extraordinary companies and saved millions of lives, helped bring education to the masses and created the greatest of countries.

People who bring new ideas to the meeting or conference call are invariably heroes who help all others become better, stronger, faster, and more enthusiastic. Although it may sound like trivial, new ideas and new information are also a welcome bit of workplace entertainment that gets others thinking and engaging. You can be one of these idea people and it is an outstanding way to differentiate yourself early in your career.

I learned this lesson when I was managing our relationship at one of our largest strategic customer accounts in the Pacific Northwest. We wanted to keep our ear to the ground and have a great understanding of their priorities and projects. This meant that we wanted to find reasons to be onsite, in status meetings at least monthly, but optimally, more often than that. The customer team members, on the other hand, knew full well that these status calls could easily be handled with a telephone conference call, saving them and us a lot of time. We made it our priority to brainstorm new ideas, new insights, and new info to share at each meeting. We spent at least a half day preparing and researching for each status meeting. The effort to inform and entertain paid off: we managed to keep our onsite meeting in place, every third week, for five years running. Of course, once in the headquarters and past security, we spent the rest of the day dropping by people's offices and getting involved in any way that we could, resulting in at least $15M in additional, ancillary business.

It is important to first understand the situation well. Rarely are people completely accepting of ideas from the person who just showed up yesterday. How long you have to be in a group and the time it takes to establish your credibility varies. In a college class, it might be quick — perhaps a week or two — while at some workplaces it might take a much longer time. What your idea is matters a lot — for example, you might have a great idea to improve the break room that can be offered early on, as you have credibility at that coffee corner level, but your idea for how to improve the manufacturing process should probably wait until you understand how it evolved over the last number of years and all the things that have been tried and learned over the last decade.

Creativity is a process of thinking about and reconnecting existing ideas to new variants. The easiest way to become more creative is to read more, jotting down your thoughts in an idea journal. Make a habit of jotting down every problem that you see and brainstorm for ideas — large and small — especially out-of-the-box ideas to solve any problems you observe. Like the rest of [ESC][AVG], becoming a creative problem solver is a matter of getting into a habit of spotting problems and brainstorming ideas that might solve them.

Experiment, invent, design, create. Combine ideas, share them, test them. Fresh ideas help you get in any door. The one-liner "I wanted to share an idea I have that I believe might help..." opens a lot of doors and often helps you start a new relationship. Another great approach is "I have some feedback for you if you are interested..." which seems to open many doors.

Consider establishing and having a digital idea board where you dump your ideas for later review and consideration. I currently use mindmeister.com which allows for the creation of outline mind maps that let you drag and drop stuff all over a large, practically unlimited digital whiteboard in the cloud.

Discuss ideas with others with the goal of getting different perspectives and additional input — especially people who are different than you. This may sound like a small idea, but teams where everyone is the same gender and age are far less creative than when a team is more diverse. Above all, I believe that reading a lot is the best catalyst for idea generation. Read a mix of fiction and non-fiction. Don't make the mistake of keeping all your ideas secret as though the ideas are all gold that must be hoarded and patented. Most people get farther in life sharing and creating ideas together. Granted, if you invent cold fusion that solves the need for fossil fuels, get a lawyer and patent that, but those ideas are exceptionally rare.

The bottom line is you will become a creative idea hero if you make the effort to build the discipline, to write it all down in your idea repository, to build the habit into second nature for you. You have the power to choose and ultimately decide what your mind will focus on, and what it will become.

Chapter 15 | Give the Gifts that Matter

Authentic, well thought out, relevant generosity helps establish authentic relationships and often, makes the giver as happy as the receiver. When you add value to a person's life, you will find that you will have established a connection that is far more likely to stand the test of time.

Most people appreciate gifts of ideas, inspiration, and time much more than simple gifts of wine and other worldly stuff. If you know what a person is interested in, you have a great leg up on what he or she would appreciate. For example, if I were to find out that Nick is interested in kiteboarding, it would be a nice gift of information to let him know of a kite-boarding event happening in a few months nearby. Give gifts of ideas, inspiration, and time freely and often. They are the most sincere gifts of our information age. That doesn't mean you don't bring a standard gift when invited to someone's house for dinner. Absolutely follow well-honed customs too.

Building the habit of paying attention and then connecting the dots is much like the other techniques of [ESC][AVG]. It starts with asking the right questions, listening well, asking open-ended follow-up questions, and writing down the details discovered in your permanotes.

Inspiration is one of the greatest gifts you can give — combining an idea with action and with potential impact. An amazing goal is to strive to inspire one person each week of your life. Keep a list of people you would like to inspire. Keep a log, perhaps on a dedicated calendar that makes it easy to see your track record over time in a familiar way.

The web has made giving these gifts that matter easier than ever before. I discovered that I could easily use my stock brokerage account watch list capabilities and other accounts such as Yahoo Finance and Google Finance to monitor the news around certain companies. In just a few minutes each morning, I scan the headlines for stories that might be interesting to my customer contacts and sales team contacts. If I find one, I use email to fire off a "saw this article / thought you might find it interesting" note to a contact. I found over time that it raised my status from casual acquaintance to a person who is conscious of what matters to my contact and clearly out for their best interest. We live in an information glut where most people can't find the signal hidden in all the digital noise. Curators are always welcome.

A word of warning: Never offer a gift of information, time, or inspiration when asking for anything for yourself. People will immediately conclude that you want a quid pro quo response from them, which will make your gift not authentic and unappreciated.

This quid pro quo phenomenon can also work in your favor, if your goal is to build better relationships. In the back of everyone's head is a favors given / favors received tally. If you want to build a better relationship with someone you don't know well, ask the person to do you a relatively easy favor and importantly, call it a favor by name. Often, that person will be happy to accommodate and take comfort that you now "owe" them a favor in the future. Conversely, asking if there is something that you can do for someone is another way to get the favor game primed and flowing, although I have found that this is more difficult as people instinctively don't want to be on the "owe" side of the favors ledger. Favors pave the path to better relationships.

Finally, traditional gifts can work, but these are much trickier, because they can easily be perceived as lightweight bribes. I have given tickets to an event to someone when I could not go myself, but it's really a tricky gift that could backfire if you appear to want a future favor in return.

Chapter 16 | Years to Build, Seconds to Lose

We have discussed the need to differentiate oneself in a positive, authentic way. Trust is crucial to the success of any relationship, and the foundation to build trust is integrity. Therefore, perhaps the greatest win / win for yourself that can also serve as a cornerstone differentiator is to commit yourself to your own unshakeable, personal integrity. Think of trust as currency that takes years to build and accumulate, but only seconds to lose.

What is personal integrity? The dictionary defines integrity as "the quality of being honest and having strong moral principles; moral uprightness." An easier way to look at it is encapsulated in three short bullets inspired by Hall of Fame college football coach, Lou Holtz:

- *Do the right thing, no matter if someone is watching or not.*
- *Do what you said you will do, within the time that you said you would.*
- *Be truthful, authentic, and transparent in your thoughts, intentions, and actions.*

Choosing to be a person of unshakeable integrity is far simpler than you think, although often not easy. Uncompromising personal integrity is a magical ingredient: the differentiator that can serve as the bedrock to build a great life of success. Unquestionable integrity is a choice that anyone can make, but in truth, exceedingly few people do. Yet, when a company is looking for a leader to oversee a division, integrity is one of the most important criteria that it looks for in candidates for the position.

The truth is that we live in a desert of integrity.

One foundational aspect of integrity is telling the truth. University of Massachusetts researcher Robert Feldman conducted a study that was published in the Journal of Basic and Applied Psychology. Robert asked two strangers to have a conversation for about 10 minutes. The conversations were recorded. Afterwards, each person was asked to review the recording. Before doing so, the research participants told Feldman that they had been 100% honest in their statements. However, during the review, the subjects were surprised to discover all the little lies that were said in just 10 inconsequential conversation minutes. According to Feldman's study, 60 percent of the subjects lied at least once during the short conversation and in that span of ten minutes, subjects told an average of 2.92 false things. If 60% of people lie when it does not matter in just ten minutes of conversation, it seems logical that more than 85% will lie when there are greater incentives, and the outcome actually matters. A recent study of dating websites found that 81% of people lied about themselves while seeking a new mate and another found that 91% of college grads lied at least once on their résumé. Our world is a desert of integrity indeed.

Another example of the integrity desert is whether people steal or cheat when they have a good opportunity. The fraud prevention industry has long held to a general rule of thumb called the 10-10-80 rule. Chain retailers with lots of experience across millions of employees believe in it. The rule says 10% of people will never steal no matter what, 10% will steal at any opportunity, and the remaining 80% of employees will steal or not steal, depending on how they evaluate a particular opportunity and their chances of getting caught. Translated, this means that if you choose to live a life of integrity, you will have chosen a differentiator that only 10% of other people choose for themselves.

Integrity involves more than simply being perfectly truthful and not stealing, although these two aspects are black and white and therefore simple to measure. Keeping your promises, doing what you say you will do — no matter what it takes — is the fundamental core basis of integrity.

The choice of integrity is available to you today, and it is completely up to you. Your past matters not, on whether you live with perfect integrity going forward. You can make the wise choice to live a life of uncompromising personal integrity from this day onward.

Integrity is the raw material that leads to trust. Trust is not something you directly control but rather, it is something that you earn or lose. Trust is the other side, the other person's choice. Other people will decide to trust you, or not trust you, based on your actions, your track record, and to a much lesser extent, your words. In fact, words over a longer length of time, become inconsequential — just ask anyone whose spouse has repeatedly cheated on them.

I believe there are always moments when life will test our integrity. How we react during the test will either make us confident, resilient, and sure of our character, or it will become a moment of long-term regret.

In my case, I had sold a large technology rollout that took 26 months to complete. Halfway through, the customer's I.T. team aggressively renegotiated a price concession as the underlying system had been reduced in price from the manufacturer. In a classic case of the right hand not knowing what the left hand is doing, we invoiced the wrong amount, and their accounts payable group paid on a big delivery at the previous higher price point. No one caught it, except for me, and in truth, I caught it a year later. The result was more than a million dollars in pure profit was in our bank and over one hundred thousand in commission bonus was in my personal investment account. I went to our CFO and the head of sales to explain the situation but everyone wanted to overlook the error, justifying it on the idea that the customer would have done it to us if the error was in their favor, based on how they had played hardball during the renegotiation of a previously signed contract.

They were probably right, but 'probably' does not change the right thing to do. After a week of soul-searching, I decided to imply that some people at the customer knew of the mistake, and it was only a matter of time before it came to light, in order to get the rebate check issued. I'm not sure if my management ever believed me 100% so in truth, it may have cost me my career potential there, and it certainly hurt when I had to pay back the six digit commission. Still, I am so glad that I passed the test of integrity. It was a lonely spot to be in when everyone involved was arguing that it was a forgotten transaction at a price originally agreed, but having no regrets is priceless. The customer's CIO was quite surprised when I showed up in his office with a seven-digit check.

I believe that integrity should become one of your key differentiators. Make your word, gold. Choose to become remarkable: becoming remarkable is not a birthright. Less than 10% of people demonstrate integrity in their daily lives by avoiding all deceit. When you add in doing exactly what you said you will do, keeping all your promises and deals large and small, you will discover a world few people know and understand: you will become a person on the road to success, without the anxiety that someone might catch you in a compromising lie. Others will inevitably learn that you are the rare person who they can count on in good times and in bad, the person who will do what he or she said they would do, the person who will do the right thing every time when put in positions of greater responsibility.

An important point is that the past is the past. Most people, maybe all people, have moments of weakness that they regret. Just because you did something that you regret doesn't mean that you can't commit to a life of integrity from this day forward. You will be better off if you make that choice today.

It takes years to build up trust, fueled through uncompromising integrity, but only one weak moment to lose it. Starting today, make no decision of character that you suspect you might regret later. Gossip is one of those areas that is best to avoid, because it seems relatively benign yet runs afoul of integrity and trust. This decision to be a person of integrity who can be trusted is not optional for the person who wants top success. Things become difficult, perhaps impossible, if your outer self is not in sync with your inner self, so you have to commit fully to the goal, be willing to forgive yourself if you ever slip up, and strive to live your life the right way.

Chapter 17 | Work Harder on Yourself than on Your Job

Fifty years ago, it was normal when a person worked for one company all their life until he or she retired. Those days are long gone. Companies watch their financials like a hawk, and when expenses grow faster than revenue, or when earnings come under pressure, restructuring the organization and reductions in employees are commonly employed strategies. New leaders are appointed, and new leaders are expected to shake things up, to do things differently. As a result, people today change jobs often.

Above average achievers often believe that getting laid-off is something that can happen to average colleagues but not to them. Unfortunately, corporations, to not get sued for any kind of discrimination, will throw aside great talent from time to time in order to follow a rule that passes the legal anti-discrimination guidelines. A perfect example of a blanket rule is "we have decided to lay-off all employees with less than 5 years with the company in every state but California." That arbitrary rule that ignored merit ejected me out of a company, right after I blew out my quota and earned the Winners Club trip to Paris. Great talent or not, your ejection seat can get triggered, so it pays to always be prepared, and to not take it personally.

The only way — let me repeat — the only way — to have a lot of options and to land on your feet, no matter the challenging moment, is to become smarter, better, more capable, better networked, and more multifaceted every month. People who think in terms of making an effort to get better "next year" rarely do get better. Getting better must be an every week thing.

Outside the workplace setting, getting better is just as important if not more so. Health is a prime example. If you are not staying mentally fit, or spiritually fit, or physically fit, it is only a matter of time before the wheels come off and the quality of your entire life takes a dive. If you are not working on your network of genuine friendships, getting better by helping others when they need help, inspiring others when they need inspiration, listening to others when they need a friend, you will find only casual acquaintances when you need that kindness and understanding.

The four primary aspects to focusing on improvement of self, improvement that matters in the long run are mental, physical, spiritual, and social.

On the mental front, college, if it did its job, programmed you to learn more efficiently and it taught you how to learn almost anything. It did not teach you everything that you need to know — in fact, it probably taught you just enough of the terminology and concepts so that you can hit the ground running without your new coworkers looking at you as clueless. You have built connectors in your brain that hopefully will attach to topics that come up, enabling you to 'fake it until you make it' while people are still giving you the benefit of the doubt.

If your school overachieved, it taught you to better control and program your mind, to decide what you want to think about and importantly, what you don't want to think about, what you decide to make part of your own operating system, and what you decide should not be part of your daily consciousness and subconsciousness. Few are that lucky, but know that getting to this introspective state will help you immensely. It all starts with choice and building your habits.

The late author David Foster Wallace gave one of the most insightful commencement addresses of recent times on this concept. Video of the speech does not seem to exist, but there is written text and audio on YouTube. If you would like to listen, this link will connect you: escavg.com/dfw

Staying sharp and improving mentally requires understanding that there is so much to learn, staying curious, questioning everything, developing mentors, continuing to learn, and deciding what you want to learn for yourself. Always ask why — why always matters the most — seek to understand. Google will often find you what happened and how it happened, but rarely is the true "why" that easy, and often, it will only be one opinion from one perspective. Keep a journal to learn over the years.

There are great hacks to help you learn and become more worldly while gaining the perspective of others. I personally think watching one TED video per day is brilliant, especially if you make some notes — the notes are what will add it to your idea bank for the longer term. If that sounds like too much commitment, consider one TED video each Saturday and Sunday — creating good habits is the secret to becoming a greater success. Reading books is essential and conversely, binging less television. In this age, there are plenty of ways, but you must build the habit as habitualizing mental improvement doesn't work if you must consciously decide and use lots of will power to make it fit your schedule.

One of the areas most average people don't work hard enough on is improving their ability to communicate effectively, to persuade others of ideas. If you learn how to become top 5% compelling and captivating, your odds of success skyrocket. The better you become at being persuasive, the more likely you are to make a positive impact, to be memorable, to help others, and, if the planets align, to advance to positions of greater responsibility. Communication comes in many forms and it pays to become excellent and highly-effective in all of them.

Rule number one of transforming your approach and becoming persuasive: You will not win your argument and persuade anyone by telling them that they are wrong in a head-on fashion. A more likely path is to understand the other person's point of view, get to a point in the conversation where you are both exploring the facts, the science, the data, and then end up with a collaborative solution to the challenge at hand. In America today, the Democrats "tell" the Republicans that they are completely wrong and vice-versa. No one budges in this scenario. Success comes when you learn how to effectively get to the desired result, helping people convince themselves in the end.

Creating a compelling presentation, white paper brief, blog post, video, or short-form email is not as hard and mysterious as most people believe. A big part of the problem is that it is challenging to rise above the constant noise, to create and deliver an outstanding, memorable presentation in a noisy, crowded, distracted, multi-media world that we live within.

Once you have a rough draft outline, there are ten checklist items that you can use to improve the story. A lot goes into rising several deviations above the level of the average presentation.

Fine-tuning details aside, most of the items for creating a compelling and captivating message can be easily baked into your effort if you follow a specific, proven formula, a checklist recipe for greater effectiveness. You must be willing to put in the work — to take your presentation that you thought was done and re-engineer it for a week or more — and then practice your honed message once it passes the checklist test as no one "kills it" the first few times he or she presents it — but if you do, I believe you will be able to achieve top 10% presentation messaging and become more compelling and memorable. Always remember that the Beatles played 'Hey, Jude' hundreds of times for live audiences, gathering feedback and making adjustments, before it became a global hit.

I have invested years creating a checklist that works, coaching others on how to improve their message, and of course, applying these principles to my own presentations. If you would like a short whitepaper that discusses my checklist, please send me a note by visiting escavg.com/checklist.

Becoming better at the delivery of your presentation takes time. Some crucial aspects take a lot of practice and are quite nuanced — for example, does the presenter achieve a personal connection to the audience even though he is speaking to a room of 300, or she is speaking over Zoom or Teams to a crowd of 1,000? Details include the ability to command attention, to make a positive first impression in seconds, to appeal to the senses despite the distance. Many of these nuances have to do with one's voice modulation, facial expressions, and body language, things that take time, coaching, experience, and effort to adjust and improve. Julian Treasure offers food for thought during his speech at TED.

Practice matters a lot. More specifically, perfect practice matters a lot. You must strive for your utmost during practice to get a great result. TED.com has their presenters practice and get coaching for months before the person lands on stage in front of a big audience. Often, you don't have the time to practice hundreds of times but be sure to practice at least 3-5 times before game day. To be clear, 3-5 times is the minimum, and it is probably not enough, but the average person practices less than that. If you want to be extraordinary, start weeks early, and practice way more, in front of some mentors or coaches or on your laptop's video camera. There is no substitute for investing the time and doing the work.

Lastly, consider joining Toastmasters to simply work on your speaking cadence and thinking on your feet without notes. Practice matters, not just of the topic you are presenting today, but practice in general. I joined Toastmasters twice, once early in my career and then again much later. Each time, I found the practice and the exercises helped me reach a new level. The more you practice, the better you become.

Outside of persuading people in larger settings, the real-world is mostly smaller meetings. An important habit to get into is taking better notes of each meeting than most of the average colleagues do, saving those notes in a great permanotes system that stays with you even if you change companies, and volunteering to be the person who summarizes the meeting on email for others. Why? Because the person with the pen has extraordinary power to put their own priorities, their own angles, into the final record and influence next actions. No one normally fights to be the person who sends the note — but that little effort helps you succeed, and you are probably going to take notes anyway. To that end, practicing writing succinctly and effectively pays great dividends.

Health and physical fitness can't be taken for granted. Lots of people prioritize their career's work only to have their life get shredded when they have a coronary event at 49. Achieving decent health for most people is not terribly difficult but you have to make it a habit as well, because great health will never be achieved in herculean bursts and if you must expend daily conscious will power.

Health and weight are closely related. Yes, of course there are people with medical conditions. Yes, there are people with genetic traits toward weight or health in general. I know that I sometimes come across a bit hard-ass and that is not my intent. My mom's life was suddenly cut short by a genetic flaw that resulted in an unexpected brain aneurysm that had nothing to do with choices she made before that fateful moment.

While I completely feel for folks that were dealt a more difficult hand in life, it doesn't take people-watching for long at the airport to realize that our society is not helping people make great choices and stay healthy. For most of us, our weight is 75% what we eat and drink, and 25% what we do physically. Some people try to cheat by working out like maniacs to allow themselves to eat and drink much more merrily, but this program does not pay off in the long run. If you want to lose some weight, a far better idea is to simply eat 20% less than you normally do while staying active, while avoiding outside-of-meals snacks. It is not super complicated: your body will balance out over time. If that doesn't tip the scales, reduce your intake bit more, eliminate your ten worst food vices, while adding more activity. Eventually, a new equilibrium is found and your body responds. It takes time and patience.

If you want to stay healthy, eat really good food, include more veggies and less fatty foods than anyone you know, keep your calorie intake below the recommended levels for your build, drink less than 6 alcoholic drinks per week, don't smoke or vape, don't touch drugs, break a sincere aerobic sweat three times per week, and lift weights three times per week on the days you are not doing aerobics. Take one day off each week. An easy way to take the guesswork out of it and make it a habit is to go aerobic/sweat on odd days, lift weights on even days, and rest on Sunday. As you get older and hit your 50's and 60's, reducing weight training to twice per week while adding one more aerobic day makes sense.

None of this will guarantee that you are about to look like a supermodel or an Olympic athlete. Today's TV and media society is so focused on visual appearance, but your goal must first and foremost be on sustainable good health. If your health becomes an issue, all other aspects of life will feel a negative impact. My dad, an above average guy with great potential, lost his high-flying career and died before he turned 60 from alcoholism.

Spiritual improvement is important too. If you are religious, church offers a lot, but don't just go through the motions, barely attending. If you put in more, you will get more out of it. If you don't lean toward religion, there are several alternatives that help you connect with the world in a spiritual way. Some people recharge by getting away from the daily hustle and bustle by embracing nature, hiking, camping, fishing, hunting, climbing, skiing, rafting, mountain biking, and more. Others engage deeply in sports and take a golf or sailing vacation for example, although most sports tend to fall in the short-term interlude bucket. Still others get away and reconnect with the world by visiting spas or meditating in gardens get-aways. I believe one of the best ways to recharge the spirit is found through helping others. Helping others is one of the most fulfilling things that we can do. Volunteering once a month will change your life.

The fourth area of self-improvement is social. Building a broad network of close friends, friends who you trust whole-heartedly, is incredibly important to living a fulfilling, successful life. Such friendships are rarer than many people appreciate. Five great, life-long friends will do more for your happiness than lots of financial riches. Choose your close friends slowly, carefully, and then don't change them out if possible. Creating a great social fabric, one that transcends time and place and space, takes genuine effort, genuine caring and love, and genuine trust. Unfortunately, most people do not have five such friendships, but instead, a lot of casual friends of convenience who vaporize when you change jobs or communities.

Continuous self-improvement — mentally, physically, spiritually, socially — is difficult but not impossible. It helps to have a mentor, a coach, that keeps you on-track. How will you get a coach? Here's a little food for thought: Even the best of the best, dominant professionals such as Tiger Woods, Lebron James, or Lionel Messi, live within this never-ending cycle of coaching. In every case, continuous improvement follows a formula of measurement, analysis, planning, practicing the new adjustments, implementation in real life situations, and then a return to measurement, as the cycle repeats. To achieve a long run of continuous improvement, coaches are always involved, and data is dutifully recorded and studied. Your chances of continuous self-improvement will improve if you figure out your coaches who can help you improve.

The bottom line is you must strive to get better, to work harder on yourself than you do on your job. It must be a balanced program that becomes habitual. Comedian, actor, and director Steve Martin nailed it when he said, *"Become so good that they can't ignore you."*

Chapter 18 | Red Pill Clarity and Time

In the blockbuster Matrix trilogy of movies that made a stunning $1.6 Billion worldwide, Morpheus offers Neo a choice of taking the red pill or the blue pill. Take the red pill and have your eyes opened, learn what the enslaving Matrix really is, or take the blue pill and return to a life of blissful ignorance with only an occasional hint that things might be different than they seem on the surface. If you have never seen the original movie, it is well worth it — two decades later, the ideas are an interesting parallel universe to life in a knowledge-based society.

The red pill offered Neo extraordinary clarity, although the clarity came with a price — Neo could never go back to the way it was before. He suddenly learns that everything he perceived as reality has been an illusion, a construct of normality injected into his mind.

There are some uncanny parallels between the movie and our lives. Many people slave away, diligently working long hours day in and day out. trying to break free to financial freedom, but most never seem to get far ahead. The realities of the bell curve dominate the landscape, with 70% of people staying within the first deviation around the norm, never escaping the grip of "slightly below average / average / slightly above average" financial and personal success. This life-near-average is because people remain in a semi-blissful state of ignorance when it comes to their single, most precious, scarcest resource.

This is your red pill clarity moment.

Many people think the most precious resource is money. It is important, it certainly helps if you have access to excess amounts of capital that you can invest, but it is not in the top three of your most precious resources for most of us. Our most precious and fleeting resource is time, assuming that you have the other two, your physical and mental health. As with any key resource, how one invests a precious resource matters a great deal.

Escaping average absolutely requires successfully navigating and mastering this key concept: Do you invest your time wisely or do you choose to spend and squander time?

Webster's dictionary defines the term 'invest' this way:

> Invest – transitive verb

> 1: to commit time or money in order to earn a future return
> 2: to make use of for future benefits of advantages (invested her time wisely)

As soon as most people get out of school and plunge into the real-world of work, the real-world Matrix, which is made up of the companies most people work for, takes over a huge slice of their time. Soon thereafter, many people cede investing their time for themselves, instead investing their time on behalf of the company. When you give the company all your best time, you are often spending nearly all your time without advancing to your own personal outlook. The spending habit spills over to "free time" — free time away from work is often spent on trivial pursuits such as sports, parties, watching TV, going to the malls, and eating. When you hit your thirties, marriage and kids often come next, and most of one's outside of work time is then spent on family events. After kids fly the nest, many wrongly believe they are too old to start much new.

It is simple: You must invest your time (and your money) wisely to get ahead and break out of the average and into the second (~15%) and third deviations ~2.5% of success. Making choices in terms of investment vs. spending changes everything regarding success. Achieving time and financial freedom, where you have greater freedom to do exactly what you want to do, is a great goal.

Time is valuable. How we invest it, matters. Time is scarce and fleeting, our most precious resource assuming health is fine. Unfortunately, most of us choose not to manage our time well.

Not all time is the same. Prime time is rare and matters the most.

By the nature of our hectic existence, each of us has little "prime" time in our daily life. Prime time is time where we are at peace but alert, focused, our senses heightened, our thoughts clear and distraction free. Some new-age gurus call it 'being in the zone' or in a state of flow. In this state, a person is often able to create new things, distill true meaning, plan with clarity, and make important progress on strategic projects.

The world around us conspires to grab a person's prime time hours for use on other people's urgencies and agendas — I call it the great Urgency Conspiracy. Many people deny that they are firmly in the grip of the Urgency Conspiracy, but most people are infected.

Although some people won't make the effort, I recommend that you track how you use your time over the next two weeks and dutifully record what happens, half hour by half hour. If you complete this experiment, I believe you will come to the following conclusions:

- Few events are pre-planned unless it is a meeting with other people.
- You spend your best prime time hours on other people's agenda items right now.
- You spend little time – if any – thinking strategically.
- You use little time – if any – improving yourself and your capabilities and knowledge.
- You invest exceptionally little time – if any – making progress on a project that could be considered an important longer-term mission.

- You tend to over-promise and over-commit to the point of capacity. When something goes wrong – and something often does – you sacrifice any personal time you have to make up for the shortfall in available hours.

We are surrounded by a multitude of outside influences. This is not new, as people were surrounded back in the 60's 70's, 80's, and 90's too. However, in the last decades, there has been a massive, unhealthy shift in people's expectations of real-time / right-now urgency and demands for an immediate response on all matters, many of which are not urgent at all. The acceleration started with 'when it positively needs to be there overnight' Federal Express followed by fax. Soon, we had voicemail and paging, then email, then instant messaging, and now instant Twitter and Facebook and especially SMS texting — all have changed everyone's real-time expectations. The more one participates in the real-time world, the more it accelerates. The urgency conspiracy is spreading like a highly contagious airborne virus. It truly infects those who are proud of their multi-tasking abilities. The word of the day, every day, is busy.

Sadly, when we occasionally receive a gift of unexpected free prime time, we are usually not ready to do something good with it. Instead, we grab the smartphone and log-on to check emails, surf websites, check out Facebook to see what our buddies are doing or eating, or read news feeds. When was the last time you saw a news story, or a tweet, or a Facebook entry that changed your life and mattered 3 weeks later? When was the last time you read a text message that mattered 3 weeks later? We have become junkies for real-time, but mostly useless, information.

Our fast-paced lives can be compared to professional soccer. When you have the ball, the defense is right on top of you, giving you no time to think, no time to look up, no time to make a good pass. The best pros, the select few with long all-star careers, are the ones that find tricks that can create some time and space to set up the creative play that winds up scoring and winning the game at the critical juncture.

You must reclaim your prime time in your daily life and invest it wisely. Most of us will never have more than a couple of hours each day of prime time. But if you make space to think, if you set appointments on your calendar to not get interrupted while you work on the important project that matters to you, you will find that you will accomplish your strategic goals and create things of lasting value, instead of just staying busy on faux urgent matters.

Building a good habit takes 6 - 12 sincere weeks and a great trigger. Start small — reclaim 30 minutes of prime time each day by making an appointment with yourself — 30 minutes is surely not too much to ask. Plan those 30 minutes at a time like 10 am when you are typically fresh, alert, and attentive. Pre-plan what you will work on during that 30 minutes of prime time and focus on this one objective. Put the smartphone on silent for that 30 minutes, or better yet, leave it in another room. Disconnect from all your usual sources and feeds. Leave the office if you must, or at least close your door. Consider closing interrupter apps like email. If you follow this habit for one month, you will discover pre-planned prime time is not only possible, but critical. Then step up to two 30-minute appointments, pre-planned each day, for the next month. Explore how far investing time wisely can take you.

A person who reserves and invests just one or two hours of prime time each day will complete a novel in about a year; or create a great new website; or develop a new app while learning JavaScript; or build a pretty little gazebo in your backyard; or learn to fly a plane; or record a video blog for your kids when they are grown and you are gone; or begin to speak French. What can you create or accomplish, of lasting long-term value, if you stop living exclusively to the busy drumbeat of other people's urgencies?

You have now taken the red pill and you have clarity. Reclaim at least one hour per day of prime time for your own goals and invest it wisely.

Time is free, but it is priceless: you can't own it, but you can invest it, or spend it, or waste it. Plan, then stick to your plans, or lose the time that you have been given.

Chapter 19 | Invent, Innovate, Initiate

An important difference between good success and great success is found in taking unexpected initiative and creating something excitingly novel. This plays out at every level, from advancing quickly as an employee, to starting a new company, to creating new art that changes people's perspective. While doing the same thing 10% better will help you escape average, creating a new thing that makes the old thing yesterday's news will propel you to higher heights.

I have found over the years that creativity works like any muscle in your body. If you exercise it, if you look for moments to use it, if you take some risks and try new things, if you create outlines, whiteboards, and post-it walls, you will become more creative and build a reputation of creativity and initiative. There are interesting side benefits too: Creativity often is a fountain of youth that helps a person's enthusiasm for life, which keeps them young, hungry, motivated, and clearly differentiates them from others.

Take a quick inventory. What did you create this month, or what new initiative did you take? If the answer is nothing, what about last month? Or the month before. If the answer remains nothing new, this is the moment that you must recognize the dangerous thin ice upon which you stand. Average people don't take much initiative. Extraordinary people do.

A seemingly innocuous habit, a habit that I had myself, can hamstring our chances of success. I dreamt up hundreds of ideas in my twenties and thirties, sharing them freely with my friends and associates. The problem happens when you have a cool, new idea and you basically get positive acknowledgement and feedback for the idea. Over time, I realized that the excitement and feedback for the idea basically gave me a warm glow too early in the process. Once you got that positive feedback, doing the work on the idea became more of a chore for the accolades had already come and gone.

Actions speak louder than words. Most people talk about what they plan to do before they start. Many people then don't follow-through or get talked out of their plan. It is much better to take decisive action and later tell others when you have finished. If you decide to be a creative spark at work, doing it before talking is best. That way, if it doesn't work out, you can learn but don't always have to highlight setbacks.

Please realize that many managers and VPs are no longer risk takers. They have already made the jump into higher pay grades and are usually in a latter season of their life, full of responsibilities. While it is important to balance integrity and be a person who is truly trusted, it is sometimes better to innovate and ask for forgiveness than it is to ask for permission, because average people and average managers don't often understand the value of taking prudent risks or the courage required to go against the status quo. Teams often need a person who is the creative spark that ignites progress. Become the spark on your team, be the person who helps your entire team succeed, and you will rise over time. Fortune favors the bold.

Taking initiative matters both in the microcosm of an individual job and the macrocosm of starting a new company or inventing a new product.

Home run success is quite different from top 15% success. The habits and disciplines of the [ESC][AVG] offer the right way to escape average. Becoming a top 15% success positions a person to go farther under the right circumstances at the right time — top 2% success is a much more lavish neighborhood than top 5%, and top 1% is yet another major click. But it would be remiss to not mention the outsized role taking initiative and creating new stuff plays in home run (top 0.00001%) successes.

Nearly every home run success in the world is based on taking initiative and creating something that did not exist before. Home runs rarely belong to a person who was hired at the lowest rung of an organization and worked his way up to the top like Doug McMillon has at Walmart. Doug is now worth more than $100M, but that still pales compared to the founder money of Larry Ellison, Elon Musk, Bill Gates, Steve Jobs, Mark Zuckerberg, Oprah Winfrey, Sara Blakeney, or Richard Branson. Warren Buffet might be the most notable exception to this formula as he executed an investment discipline that many knew. Warren evolved that discipline and simply did it better and with far more patience than others could manage.

In an upcoming chapter, I will discuss that capitalism rewards capitalists. Capitalists who own large shares of financially successful enterprises do really well. Successful companies are those that tend to solve important needs and valuable problems.

It has never been easier to create a new megacompany than it is today. Vast fortunes have been created without the investment of lots of financial capital: the Kardashians, Oprah, Michael Jordan, Jerry Seinfeld, Mark Cuban, Jay Z, and others all became crazy rich with relatively little financial capital invested. Recent history has illustrated that a modern world rewards those who create new stuff, new solutions, new businesses, new songs, new movies, new whatever.

If you want to take the principles of [ESC][AVG] and end up with a home run, the path is to be creative, take action, find the white space, and deliver what the world wants or needs. Your odds are long, but there is no doubt that someone will do it. Why not you?

In the end, few things have propelled my personal success more than becoming Big-Idea-Rob, and then acting on a good number of my ideas. When I outlined the need to differentiate yourself, I didn't share that ideas, initiative, and optimism are my personal big three differences. There is no substitute for initiative and decisive action. Initiative is opportunities, planning, and trailblazing action all in one. Talk is cheap, action is priceless. I can promise you that this is a winning combination.

Chapter 20 | Nothing Ventured, Nothing Gained

Nothing ventured, nothing gained. Four words that have survived nearly 700 years and 28 generations of humans since the mid-1300's. Why? Any essential truth, thrives.

There are extraordinary opportunities available to all of us. We live at an amazing time, a time of fantastic and rapid change, a time that lets some people rise quickly in prosperity. I believe that the opportunities to achieve whatever one wants to achieve are nearly limitless.

Of course, there are certain people who are in better positions on the starting line, people who are born into the right family at the right time or get a one-in-a-lifetime lucky break, but making the right decisions and taking the right chances has propelled many who started in seemingly disadvantaged beginnings.

My grandparents arrived with my eight-year-old mom as immigrants to America at the end of World War II without a penny to their name, unable to speak more than a few hundred words of English. The first six years of my mom's life were nothing but running, ducking, and trying to stay alive. Their village in Lithuania had been pummeled first by the Germans and then by the Russians. Fate was not kind to a small country smack dab between two military powerhouses with thousands of tanks. My grandfather went to work in Chicago's railyards while my grandmother sewed pockets for men's suits. Just a decade later, they managed to put my mom through dental school and were so proud when she graduated as the only woman in a class of ~100 men.

Unfortunately, many people don't see unlimited opportunities, or don't embrace a specific opportunity, because they can't see past the risks that must be taken. Risk is ever-present, and it is one of the primary reasons that many people settle for a small life, doing small things, complaining about small hurts and offenses.

Twenty-somethings have a great advantage over most of the working population. If they grew up in an optimistic home, they believe that they can conquer the world, they have little if anything to lose, they don't yet listen to, or at least adhere to, the often faulty, limited "wisdom" of their elders, and they have had few disheartening experiences. These are the reasons most tech start-ups are fueled by young adults.

As we get older, people tend to take less and less risk. This risk aversion invades most of the facets of a person's life: financial, emotional, professional, psychological, personal, you name it. Yet the core truth of "nothing ventured, nothing gained" rules nearly every facet of life.

By the time people hit their 40's, most don't want to take any chances. This is often a mistake. Without accepting risk, all you can expect is a mediocre return following the path of the risk-free herd. When you embrace smart risks, you expand your possibilities and your life.

Overcoming the fear of risk is possible and comes from learning and understanding probability better than the average person. Risk is simply half of the equation: once a person learns to evaluate risk clearly, in relation to probable return, she can start making educated decisions regarding the worthiness of any endeavor.

It is easiest to understand risk vs. return in simple betting. If someone offers you 3:1 odds on the flip of a quarter, it becomes a good bet – in other words a risk worth taking, because the quarter flip will win 50/50 over time. On a dollar bet, you would get paid $3 the 50% of the time that you win but lose only $1 the 50% of the time you would lose. The longer you play this game, the greater your returns become.

If you absolutely hated math word problems in college, please skip the next paragraph. I get it – some people are just not math people and this stuff will sound like *"one train left Indianapolis heading east at 60 mph while another train left Philly at 40 mph…"* - but I think the lesson is worth the "math" risk.

Smartly gauging risk vs. reward pays off in life. If you invest $1,000 in a growing, successful company that has a current price to earnings (P/E) ratio of 10, a historical low for the stock because of a short-term sell-off, while all its close competitors have P/E's of 25 – barring any skeletons in the closet, you generally have taken a good bet – odds are much better that your stock will appreciate to $2,500 (or perhaps more if earnings grow over time) rather than falling to $500 in the future. You can further mitigate the risk by investing $1,000 in 10 companies in similar scenarios. Even if you are wrong on 5 of 10 — where 3 of them get halved while 2 tread water and stay at the price paid — if the other five do move up to their historical P/E, your final tally would be $16,000 on a $10,000 in investments, or a 60% return. If you leave that $10,000 in a money market account at Bank of America, the earnings from interest rates have been meager and barely keeping up with price inflation.

Check out my blog post with simple charts that talks through *"Everything you need to know about the stock market in just three pages"* here: escavg.com/stocks

Many people never overcome their fear of perceived risk. My suggestion is start small and gain momentum gradually. A big misconception is that those who take risks are fearless. This is not true. People who take prudent risks, after weighing the probable rewards, are courageous and smart.

I know that some of my advice sometimes comes across a little hard ass, a little bit too much like the *"Just Do It"* Nike tagline. I know that I sometimes sound like this because it has worked for me, numerous times, over the years. After all the planning, after all the prep, after the T charts of benefits versus potential risks, there is often a moment when I had to simply decide and to be "all in" from that moment forward. I get that *"just do it"* doesn't work for everyone, or in every situation, but it has worked for me to find the courage to go "all in" and make the valiant effort.

How a person finds the courage to act at the crossroads is different for different people. I think I decide to be courageous because ultimately, I want to have no regrets. Regret is often the product of not taking a chance, not embracing an opportunity, when we had it. While people offer a lot of excuses for why they missed out as they express regrets, the underlying truth is most often a failure of courage. If you are not making mistakes, it is a clear indicator that you are not trying enough new things. But it takes courage to try anything new, to embark on any exciting new journey, to try a road less traveled by the rest of the human herd.

The hardest step is always the first — getting started comes before getting motivated — and getting started takes courage.

Nothing gets in people's way more often than fears, but fears are usually quite silly once one looks back on them and sees them for what they really are. It is often more than just the fear of failure that prevents people from trying the new. Others fear success, for with success comes far greater responsibility. Others yet fear change or the unknown, simply because they assume that the unknown is worse than where they are today. Small-minded people fear people who are not like them, or people who think differently than them. In every case, those who decide to risk in the face of small fears or large fears, expand their lives and their horizons. This is courage and like every key to success, courage can be learned, courage can be practiced, courage can be expanded through experiences.

This is not to say that all fear is bad. Fear is what drives prudent decision-making, in other words balancing the chance of success versus the chance of failure. But those without courage allow themselves to become paralyzed. Fear prevents so many things that are good. A person with a fear of rejection doesn't stick their hand out and introduce themselves to new people. Similar fears convince people to not try out for the team, to not run for class president, to not put in for that promotion, to not decide to have kids, to not be all they can be. In each of these cases, the upside potential usually outweighs the downside risk but those who have not developed the courage to take risks, shrink away from opportunities.

All the great leaders of the last century have observed the extraordinary importance of courage. Winston Churchill proclaimed, *"Courage is the first of the human qualities because it is the quality that guarantees all the others."* He is right. I have often written about the crucial importance of integrity. Is it possible to be a person of integrity if you do not have the courage to stand up for what you believe is right? Is it possible to have extraordinary character if you don't have the courage to stand up to peer pressure? Your faith will be tested, as will your sense of duty. Even your purpose will be questioned, and you will have to have the courage to swim against the ever-changing winds of "popular" thinking.

Courage takes practice. One doesn't typically have the courage to speak in front of an audience of thousands if they have never spoken in front of an audience of five, then ten, then thirty. One doesn't step onto a basketball court and hit two game winning free-throws unless they have played thousands of games first. The trick is to take every small opportunity you can, at least every one that makes prudent sense along the road of life, so that when the time comes, you have the experience and the courage to give it your best shot.

Preparation may not put you completely over the top, but it makes that last bit of courage far easier to muster. Courage allows a person to become decisive, to grab opportunities that others do not, to take chances when the odds are good.

As always, think plans through on paper. Ink and paper are magical when striving to be more logical. Ask mentors to review your plans.

Most people don't get this far, but the better your plan, the more likely you are to accurately estimate the risk versus possible return.

It is incredibly important that a person learns to embrace prudent calculated risk during his entire life, learning from experiences as he or she grows older. There are always risks worth taking, and when you are 40, 50, or 60, you have a much broader base of experience, connections, and resources than when you were but 22. The idea is not to put more than you can afford to lose in any one investment or idea.

My discussion took a financial turn because it is easy to illustrate with numbers, but taking prudent risks is just as vital on your emotional, professional, personal, and psychological facets of life. There will be a few rare moments in life when you must take a prudent risk and stand up to bullies — you can't always avoid conflict. If you come up with a great idea that is worthy at work, take the risk and earn a meeting with your own CEO. Pitch it! You might just make Executive VP after all. Search for new jobs and land that job interview. Ask that girl out. Go ahead and volunteer when they ask. Speak up at the community meeting. Try helping at the local soup kitchen or Meals-on-Wheels or Big Brothers Big Sisters! Start that little business on the side and stick to the project to the finish line. Always remember that it helps to fail spectacularly from time to time to learn and become extraordinary in the end.

One of my own spectacular failures was when I left flat-line-revenue NCR for a medium-sized printing and packaging company in Dallas. I had met the CEO from playing basketball at a park near downtown and we became friends. John decided to recruit me although he didn't have a clear role or vision for how I would help. By my late twenties, I thought my destiny was to have my own company and John offered me leadership over his floundering packaging division. It seemed like what I needed to learn how to turn around a struggling business, but I quickly found out that the leap took me to a place where I had exactly zero experience. I was not a manufacturing guy, I had never dealt with labor force problems, and I didn't have a clear vision on what to do to improve Packaging. Worse yet, I didn't jump in with all-in commitment but rather approached it with a dip-a-toe-in-the-water attitude.

In less than a year, I pivoted and was back in major account technology sales, licking my wounds and for the first time, understanding my personal capabilities and the crucial requirement for "all-in" a bit more clearly. I don't regret the mistake, and believe me, it was a mistake. It was a great lesson to learn — go to a place where you have clear value-add and decent fit — and a lesson in humility as well. Another small but valuable lesson learned was to not tell your CEO that you are going to leave, before you have a new gig. I know it sounds obvious now, but it felt like the right thing to do then. It resulted in my jumping to the first place I could get hired, just to get out of the situation I was suddenly in. Luckily, I was fortunate and landed on my feet, but luck alone is no substitute for a good plan.

Wayne Gretzky, who is perhaps the greatest hockey player ever, was right when he said,
> *"You miss 100% of the shots you don't take."*

Here's my Nike perspective coming out again. The world can be your oyster if you embrace it. Envision yourself courageous. Take smart risks. Embrace opportunities with little hesitation. Most importantly, realize that courage requires practice. Start with small steps, just do it one small step at a time, and you will find your own way to be courageous, and to become all that you can be. Life is not about beating someone else. In truth, success is about becoming the best person that you can be, and courage is what helps you live large.

Chapter 21 | No Gold Medal for Starting the Race

No one ever succeeded because of how many projects they started but then abandoned unfinished. While getting started is important, in truth, finishing is what matters most.

In this day of exponential networking and explosive knowledge-sharing growth, ideas multiply like rabbits. It is all too easy to start a new website, form a new business, create a new venture, and become available to much of the planet. But for all the ease of the start, finishing is nearly as difficult as it has always been. Note that in many ventures, there is a long series of finish lines, not just one. Versions one, two, and three rarely take the world by storm. If you look closely, most overnight successes required years getting to the self-sustaining, unstoppable momentum finish line.

If you want to change your trajectory, action is required. Doing nothing accomplishes nothing. Nothing great happens without optimism, decisive action, tenacity, and patience. The last two, tenacity and patience, are what it takes to finish. In the long run, finishing is the only thing that matters.

Before you start something new, I suggest weighing all your options and planning as much as possible on paper, running your plans through a gauntlet of positive, optimistic mentors. Plan well, which means creating not only Plan A, but Plan B and C too. Plan with enough detail. The true value of planning is not that every step will go according to plan — it will not — but rather that you think things through with logic in meticulous detail and then commit your thoughts to paper. A plan gives you a skeleton to solicit the feedback of others, it helps you remember your initial assumptions, it helps you pivot, to adapt and overcome, when a pivot is needed.

If you are having trouble with creating a great plan, try this trick — plan the project backwards. Start with the end in mind — the "what" you will accomplish. Then clearly write down "why" you want it and "why" it is important. The "why" gives goals life, and fuels tenacity. Then, working backwards, discern all the detailed first down milestones (the "how") that you must accomplish to get to that endpoint. I personally prefer outliner tools to do this — my current favorites are OmniOutliner on the Mac and MindMeister in the Cloud — but index cards and post-it sticky notes also work well.

Even though finishing is what counts, simply getting started often trips people up. Many people tend to think too much and do too little. Everyone is talking about "being motivated", "getting motivated" or "lacking motivation" yet sit on their duffs watching T.V. for several hours each day.

Most everyone has this motivation formula reversed. The truth is that getting started usually comes before getting motivated.

How many times do you hear "*I need to find a better job*" — but when you poke a bit with a few more questions, you find out that the person has no updated resume and has not lifted a finger to look for a better job? How often do you hear "*I need to lose twenty pounds*" or "*I need to go to the gym more often*" but "*I can't find the motivation.*" How many salespeople want bigger commissions but have not increased the pace and quality of their sales efforts? How many people say they want to improve their investing knowledge but have not read a single book about investing in over a decade because they say that they "*can't get excited*" about the topic?

Getting out of the planning stage and launching with massive, committed action is important. You must decide that when you look in the mirror, you see yourself as a person of action. Acta non verba. The truth is that if you:

- Look for that better job and you will find one.
- Go to the gym and you will workout.

- Download a calorie tracker app on your iPhone, start using it before each meal for six weeks, and you will lose weight.
- Read *The Little Book that Still Beats the Market* or the classic *The Richest Man in Babylon* on your Kindle while walking on the treadmill and you will be closer to financial investing.
- Take a lesson or two, and you will be snowboarding.
- Attend a few weeks of classes and you will find that Spanish is not so hard.
- Write the first ten pages of your novel and the next twenty pages will flow more easily.

Action matters. What's the one thing you have been talking about doing but have whined about finding the motivation? No more whining! Every journey, every adventure starts with a single step. Get started today. Take that first step and then a second.

I am as guilty as anyone for starting far too many projects and not seeing many of them through to the finish line. I flew to Seattle and Portland in the 80's to study Starbucks and other coffee purveyors in the Pacific Northwest, long before Starbucks had locations in Dallas, but then didn't pull the trigger on my first location lease and the idea went nowhere after years of planning. I spent a lot of cash on developing a sports stats application that ultimately never made it to any app store. I partnered with others to create a Management by Objectives software as a service, but it too, almost made it, but fell short after more than a year of effort. I have many more, most of which have now been finished by others.

The lesson is straightforward — nothing great happens with just a great idea and a solid start. Never forget that finishing the race, the race you have decided to run, matters most. Finishing takes grit. Finishing strong matters 100% more than starting strong.

So how do you finish? If you find yourself all over the place, starting but not finishing projects, make the decision to start less projects, pick the one with the best risk/reward potential, and concentrate your focus on one project at a time. As the saying goes, don't chase two rabbits or they will both escape.

Not only does finishing take grit, but it also invariably requires tenacity with flexibility to enable you to adapt and overcome. Assume that there will be lots of setbacks. Assume that the finish line that you think is the finish line will probably not be the end of the adventure, and that there will be unanticipated future finish lines lurking over the horizon. One great burst of energy rarely gets someone to the promised land.

One of the fairy tales that all of us heard when we were kids was the tortoise and the hare. Slow and steady tortoise one the race because she never stopped. Most projects that win the gold medal reflect that constancy of effort. That Olympic gold medalist in the 800-meter race started more than a decade earlier on some hot, dusty afternoon on the north side of Des Moines, Iowa, then practiced and practiced, and practiced some more until they stood on the medals platform in Tokyo, listening to the Stars Spangled Banner play triumphantly across the stands.

Patience has become an often overlooked virtue in this internet-connected, everything in real-time world that we live in. People often miss out of greatness because they choose to be impatient instead of patient. Extraordinary people combine continuous, persistent action with the belief and patience to let things play out. Tolstoy did not write War and Peace in just a couple of months. Michelangelo did not paint the ceiling of the Sistine Chapel in a year. James Cameron's Avatar took fifteen years from the beginning of development to the theater premier. If you are making progress, and you can see why the outcome will be great, you must have the patience and persistence to see it through.

Over time, I learned to delay and schedule other good ideas and projects until I finished the one that I was focused on this year. I realized that in all my early ventures, it wasn't the idea that was flawed but it was me. Having too many good ideas was my Achilles Heel, making it all too easy to jump on the next problem to solve that really excited me. I hope that you learn this lesson without having to go through years of suffering and mistakes as I did.

Break monster projects into do-able micro-sprints, and reserve time slots on your calendar. Celebrate measurable milestones in reasonable time. Measuring your progress matters because what gets measured gets improved. Above all, avoid multitasking — it is one of the greatest foolishness in society right now — multitasking is a sure way of not doing your best on whatever you are trying to accomplish right now.

In the end, you will discover that finishing becomes a habit too, within the people who are most successful. If finishing is the only thing that counts, finish more, finish habitually, finish like your success depends on it.

It is way too easy to let other people think — and make conclusions — for you. We are often quick to accept myths, and propagate them to others, as though they were God-given.

Myths are all around us. Here's one: We only use a small percentage of our brain. Simply not true, disproven by numerous scientific studies. But the fiction continues to swirl.

Here is another: Men and women are dramatically different. Not so much. In truth, the differences are statistically small when it comes to language ability, spatial reasoning, and many other factors, with a large percentage of women outperforming the average man on all factors except for physical strength (and vice versa on the factors where the average woman outpaces the average man).

Left-handed people are more creative. Nope. Visual learners vs auditory learners. Everyone has a major lean one direction or the other, right? No, not right. Listening to Mozart makes you smarter. All this is myth because differences that are measured and detected are negligible in scale and biased by the test itself. Flying isn't safe. Actually, it is crazy safe. Crashing is not safe — ok, that one is true.

Want another 1,000 myths busted? Watch old MythBusters episodes — I love any show that questions and tests prevailing wisdom.

Unfortunately, or fortunately, depending on your perspective, few humans question 'facts' and do their own research. The wisdom of crowds is often, not so wise. Google makes it easier than ever to try to dig one or two layers deeper — but of course, you must question the motives and perspective of the article authors you find as well. Often, one falsehood spawns dozens if not hundreds of articles and results in misled groupthink. Googling doesn't always give you deeper data, but often, it just gives you popular data of what the average person believes. AI tools that strive to only offer one answer, instead of an array, might make things worse for a while.

Why is this fortunate then? Because the quality of your decision making will be a huge factor in determining whether you become average or become extraordinary. If most people don't delve a bit deeper, if they believe false data, if they don't double-check, they are the ones likely to make the wrong decisions and stay firmly lodged in the all-too-average herd.

Critical thinkers adopt a different approach. When they hear a "fact" spoken with great authority, they realize that it is wise to question it until it stands the test. I have found that perhaps as many as 70% of boldly stated facts are tainted, or the differences exaggerated so much so that making decisions based on them is foolish. I realize that I often don't get to the absolute core truth, but thinking it through, the process itself, is always helpful in the end.

One of the "facts" I strongly disagree with is that a person "can't beat the stock market averages" so therefore, go ahead and invest in mutual funds, invest with (expensive) professional investment counselors and brokerages, and invest in exchange traded funds (ETFs). The implication is that you should simply strive to be average. The tens of thousands who push this idea make their living by selling their services to you. Because I questioned this fact, I have managed to soundly beat the S&P 500 average in 82% of the years that I have invested, and my multi-decade compounding result has handily outpaced investing in the S&P 500 ETF.

Stock investing returns, and almost everything in life, follows a normal distribution, a bell curve. It's the same as the bell curve of average success versus outlier success in life.

If you find your own way to stay above the average even by a few percentage points, your returns over 20 or 30 years will greatly outpace a person who is average, or a few points below. I believe that is possible by simply asking better questions, paying attention, and designing and following thoughtful principles in your approach. The reality of the stock market myth is that if most people believe they can't beat the markets, that improves the odds for people who believe that they can.

Investing is but one example. The vast majority of people are clueless on many important topics like "Number Needed to Treat" (NNT) ratios on any pharmaceutical product because they do not ask questions and seek to understand. The ugly truth is that most medicine does not work on most people. If you take a pill for a condition, there is a NNT that comes from drug studies, indicating how many patients with a certain condition must take the drug to result in one positive outcome. When you dig into your medicine cabinet, you might find that you are taking a medicine, often with documented side-effects, that only helps in 1 or 2 out of every 10 cases. There are billions of dollars at stake for Pfizer, AstraZeneca, and all the players in the industry. Many industries rely on big pharma to keep the money wheel spinning. Many doctors prescribe pills all too quickly, because doing so keeps patients on the hook and loyal to them. Imagine how zillions of ad dollars TV would lose if big pharma talked about the NNT rations. It is not surprising that few people are conscious of the NNT for the meds that they take. Ask questions. It matters.

Become a critical thinker, questioning everything, figuring out the source, and conducting experiments when applicable, as it opens new possibilities and new understanding. It is well worth adopting logical curiosity on every aspect of your life.

Take a few minutes to watch this doctor on a short TED video — and I think you will understand why you must decide to be a critical thinker: escavg.com/ben

I highly recommend taking Neil deGrasse Tyson's class on Masterclass.com. Neil does an amazing session that is not only entertaining but concisely illuminates why clear thought is a differentiator that all of us must pursue.

Life offers great possibilities to be an outlier if you believe you can be an outlier. How you think about everything, how aware you are of your surroundings, matters.

Chapter 23 | The WD-40 of Success

A few people succeed — not many but a few — by being
bullheaded, by being, above all else, persistent and determined, by
charging in with a battering ram and trying to break the lock, break
the hinges, and break down the door. These are the folks who tell
others that they are flat out wrong and argue vehemently until the
other people give up. Surprising as it sounds, I have seen this in
action in sales, where a customer finally submits and purchases
after the salesperson just stays after him with massive detail and
persistence until the customer waves the white flag and gives in to
the logic. Although it works occasionally, this is not recommended
because the odds of repeatable success are not favorable.

The true outliers of success develop a special WD-40 aspect to their
persona that changes the contentious nature of achieving their
goals. They work with the gears of the system, not against the
machine, but with it. This WD-40 is charisma.

Charisma is a better door opener than a battering ram, because
once the door is open, you are welcome to enter. Per the
dictionary, charisma is defined as a compelling attractiveness,
appeal, or seemingly magnetic charm that can inspire devotion
in others.

Some people seem to be born with charisma. Good looks, an easy
smile, a great sense of humor, and an abundance of emotional and
social intelligence, bundled with an innate sense of timing, all seem
God-given contributors. I believe that most people can learn how
to become much more charismatic than they are today.

Thankfully, I learned the lesson about "learning charisma" during
one memorable event. At the time, I was an ambivert — not an
introvert but definitely not an extravert either. Our work team
sponsored an event where a broad variety of people from our
customer showed up, and as fate would have it, not the folks we
knew well. I, and a few of the technical guys on my team, were fish

out of water, far more used to solving customer problems with a marker on a whiteboard than chatting over shrimp appetizers. It was astounding to watch Cal, a seasoned sales pro, save the day, going from conversation to conversation with James Bond like ease, albeit with a Texans accent. Cal went with the flow of every conversation, asked great open-ended questions, talked just enough, laughed just enough, and smiled all the time, putting everyone at ease. Cal single-handedly saved our event, and I learned that anyone could do this if he or she plunges whole-heartedly into everyone else's story.

Only a year later, I had learned the basics of what Cal did so well. It takes having a vision and understanding that there is a formula that works. Over time, I have expanded my understanding and can now adjust my level of extroverted-ness to fit every situation.

Learned charisma is achieved by reprogramming your mental operating system, just like all the habit disciplines of [ESC][AVG]. The simple truth is that people like people who are genuinely interested in them, people who like them. If you decide to take a genuine interest in all people, ask great questions, listen with your heart, smile, remember details with honest authenticity, you will quickly elevate your level of charisma. You must become interested in all, from the influential big boss to the lowly assistant to the waiter at your favorite lunch spot. Integrity is crucial. Never be fake. Authentic listening and caring is easily detected by the person who you are talking to, and if you selectively only "manage up" the org chart, the word eventually gets out that you are not what you pretend to be.

Smiling is one of the most underappreciated of talents. People like people who smile, project happiness, and laugh often. Smiling is a super-power, probably because so few people smile a lot. If you don't believe me, just go to your local Lifetime Fitness gym. If you spend an hour watching people, you will find that 90% of people rarely, if ever, smile. The same phenomenon is at play at the mall, or the airport, or any venue not serving copious amounts of beer and wine. Just watch the postage-stamp sized faces on a fifteen person zoom call. People act serious, and it nixes out their charisma. At work, people are even more serious as they strive to get ahead.

Remembering people's names is basic table stakes as you work on improving charisma. People often say *"I'm not good at remembering names"* but in truth, it is a practiced skill, and you can become good at it and make it a habit. Human nature means that everyone loves hearing their own name. People who remember your spouse's name, your kid's names, your friend's name occupy a whole other level in your book than people who don't. The good news is that there are proven, simple to practice techniques to build a great habit of remembering names, and of course, using ink, or digital ink, to make notes in your permanotes system helps a lot.

Once you have practiced and achieved the habits of an easy smile and remembering names like an elephant, the next technique that works wonders is to ask people for a bit of advice. Asking for advice communicates that you value a person's perspective and makes them feel great about your relationship.

Another level is achieved when you ask someone to do you a favor. Our society mandates that if someone does you a favor, you are indebted to do him a favor in the future. This favor-economy builds friendship. A lot of people hesitate to ask for a favor, but the top successes embrace it. Ben Franklin observed that if you ask an enemy or competitor for a favor, it often transforms the relationship from adversarial to something more favorable.

Don't shirk on praise when an authentic opportunity presents itself. People always like praise but it must make sense and be genuine. If someone tells you their story from last weekend and it makes sense in the context of the story, tell them *"that is awesome"* or *"wow, I wish I had the guts to bungee-jump, you are amazing, dude"* or whatever makes sense. Don't miss good opportunities to make people feel good about themselves.

Charismatics get people talking about their best topics. People like interactions where they get the opportunity to talk about their deepest interests — a charismatic person discovers that thread and then encourages the conversation around that thread. Even if someone's favorite topic is their problems, you must stay genuinely interested and engaged if you want to win them over and be able to influence them. Whiners and complainers make this a particular tough challenge. Ultimately, you must go out of your way to make the other person feel important, and you must do so sincerely, as it is easy to spot insincerity. All people want to be important, relevant, and respected.

A common mistake, and the reason so few people become charismatic, is that people usually are all tied up in themselves, their ego, and their desire to do the lion's share of the talking. When others are talking, most people think about what they will say next, instead of listening fully to the other person. If you develop the skill to discover what makes the other person special, if you put yourself in their shoes for just a few minutes, if you go with the flow and ask open ended questions, you will discover that charisma is indeed a secret skill that can be learned and habitualized into your own mental operating system.

It pays to study improvisation. In improv comedy, the actors / comedians are taught to listen closely to the others in the scene, openly accept whichever way the scene goes, and go with the flow. This basic idea helps when your number one goal is to have the other person talk more and take them to their favorite topics.

Above everything, you must establish credibility and trust. Credibility as a human comes from doing the right thing, treating others like you want to be treated, and showing all that you truly care. Question 'what you think you know' about someone — there is always more that you don't know than what you do know.

One bad habit that you must remove from your mental operating system is complaining. There is no such thing as a truly charismatic, optimistic person who complains often. The more you whine and complain, the less attractive you become to other people.

Lastly, many people try to become more interesting to others by relying on exaggeration about themselves and gossip about others. Both backfire and you should avoid them like the plague. Exaggeration leads to lies and more lies to cover up the initial statements. Just one lie, when discovered, ends trust, usually permanently. When you gossip, the person you are gossiping to instantly knows that you will surely gossip about her behind her back, when the opportunity presents itself. Both gossip and exaggeration ensure that you will lose whatever charisma you hope to have.

Charisma isn't everything — there are examples of people with powerful natural charisma that turned out horribly evil such as Adolf Hitler — but it is helpful because it is the great door opener to a lot of opportunity, but the rest of the [ESC][AVG] principles are far more important to plant the seeds, water the seeds, and eventually reap the harvest.

Chapter 24 | Don't Forget the Super Glue

While charisma is the WD-40 that will help you get in the door and in a better position to succeed, longer term success requires building genuine relationships where you earn the right to influence and persuade others to change their course and eventual outcomes.

We live in the hyperconnected age where communication technologies have made it easier than ever to have hundreds of lightweight, casual relationships. Lots of people understand the value of having a broad network but unfortunately, they take the easy road and network in a superficial manner. This is all too evident when you work in a large corporation. Dynamic work groups form for projects and initiatives, only to dissolve a few weeks later. People meet, collaborate a bit, and then forget each other's names within a year, even though they may remain connected on LinkedIn and can search email history only as long as they are still with the same company.

A network of casual acquaintances is not good enough. Asking the right questions, seeking to understand before you try to be understood, treating others with respect, finding out what makes someone special, figuring out what makes a person tick, and sharing personal aspects of your own are the key activities that transform a casual relationship into a good relationship. This is easiest with co-workers, but successes build good and great relationships with colleagues, customers, business partners, and social connections outside of work. It is far better to strive for one hundred good relationships than one thousand casual ones.

People who network without a genuine authentic desire to understand the other person are easy to spot. People who are genuine listen actively, go with the flow, ask great follow-on questions, and offer ideas. The less-than-genuine folks ask a couple of questions and then immediately change the subject to the topic that they would prefer to talk about.

Mutual trust is the glue required in every good or great personal and business relationship.

No great relationships are built without significant one-on-one time. If you only spend time with another person as part of a group, nothing lasting will result. Make the effort and go to lunches with people one-on-one as much as possible. Proactively invite people to meet you at Starbucks or at the local pub for a drink after work. Go play golf with someone. Go shopping at the mall. One-on-one time will improve your chances of building good, lasting relationships by a factor of ten.

My career has really been improved and accelerated — as much as 50% or more in my not-too-scientific estimate — by following a practice of getting to know people one-on-one. I kind of fell into the practice when I was assigned one large account, managed to get an unlimited access security badge, and decided to spend three days each week wandering the hallways of their headquarters. I got security badges for the others on my team and then quarterbacked our activities to build relationships. We learned about projects, what people wanted for their careers, what each person's home life was like, and who was pulling for which vendor whenever one of us had a cup of coffee in someone's office or cubicle. This kind of personal perspective never came to light when a meeting had three or more people in it. Ever since, I make a point of setting up one-on-one moments whenever possible and it never fails to improve my understanding.

Using ink, as mentioned throughout [ESC][AVG], is crucial. Once you find out some details, you must write them down in your permanotes system. Time vaporizes details so writing them down as soon as you can after you find out some gold about anyone is important. Make a practice of reviewing your notes right before you meet that person again. Remembering that her daughter had a big dance recital coming up last time you talked is the kind of detail that helps transform a passing acquaintance into a friend.

Entrepreneur, author, and corporate speaker Harvey MacKay became famous years ago for his MacKay 66 list of questions that can help any salesperson become more effective than his competitors. Harvey was dead-on right — if you can figure out even half these 66 elements about someone, your chances of forging a great relationship with him or her increases fivefold.

Over the years, using Harvey's list as inspiration, I developed two modern versions which I believe are a bit better. The essentials list are the top 20 aspects to figure out about someone first, and then the expanded list includes 100 aspects to understand someone quite thoroughly. You can take a peek and download my templates at escavg.com/20 and escavg.com/100. Building lasting relationships requires asking, learning, and remembering 90% more than the average person learns and remembers when they meet someone.

In every relationship, mutual trust is the currency that matters most. One of the golden rules of [ESC][AVG] is "never gossip and never lie" because trust evaporates the moment that anyone witnesses a person engaging in either activity. Good relationships only survive when confidential stuff remains confidential, and both people believe that they are committed to each other's best interest. One mistake that I have seen all too often is when John lies to Jim on a phone call, overheard in front of Conner. Even though John didn't lie to the Conner, Conner instantly realizes it's only a matter of time before he will be lied to by John as well.

Trust is not passive. Trust grows as two people make and keep promises to each other. No one will trust you if you do not keep your word. If you fall short, you must apologize sincerely and absolutely strive to never fall short again. This isn't baseball where three strikes get you out at the plate. In life, one strike is close to out, if not out for good. To earn trust, you must be friendly and authentic, because just keeping your promises while being grouchy and complaining will not work. Lastly, you must show trust in the other person for trust in a two-way street.

While understanding the other person's perspective is one of the most important goals when improving your relationships, you must also accurately understand yourself. Psychology gurus have spent a tremendous amount of energy trying to accomplish this goal. Myers-Briggs has risen in stature as a way to categorize personalities in about sixteen buckets. You may have run into the commercialized versions with websites such as 16personalities.com and the Enneagram Institute. A great number of psychologists have come out in opposition, saying that people's personalities are not that tidy and that Myers-Briggs based work is not accurate enough for clinical use.

Whether Myers-Briggs is breakthrough psychology or not, I believe that there is value to taking the quiz at 16personalities.com and reading the report because it helps you recognize your own tendencies, strengths, and weaknesses. Understanding oneself will help you improve over time and strengthen your relationships with others. If — and that's a big "if" because people hide many details early-on when they are getting to know you — you can accurately figure out what personality type a person is who you are building a relationship with, you can then review those personality traits and customize your approach to better fit.

Most of life is a team sport and developing ways to build quality relationships will help you succeed. In my experience, always go for quality over quantity. Quality always means sincerely looking for and finding mutually beneficial solutions to every problem. We have all heard the phrases win/win and win/lose. In every negotiation, even for something small like picking a spot for dinner, it is best to find the win/win solution where both people in the relationship walk away feeling that the scenario was fair for both parties. If you find yourself in a relationship where the other person is driven by winning while you lose, you will be best off by cutting it off and moving on.

The most successful and persuasive negotiators find ways to join the other party on the same side of the table. They transform the discussion to "how can we solve this problem together" instead of "do it my way." Relationships are best when there is mutual trust, mutual respect, and both parties feel that they are on the same side of the table, searching for a fair, win/win solution.

It takes effort to keep a good relationship alive for the longer term. Relationships are a lot like muscles. If you don't use a muscle, it tends to atrophy and will eventually disappear. Once you have established a good relationship, you must proactively work on it and make sure that the relationship stays alive and well, and if possible, grows over time.

If you meet someone who doesn't seem to trust other people, this is often an indicator that she is not trustworthy as well. Watch for this red flag because people often assume others are just like they are, and you are probably seeing a reflection of themselves when they doubt the integrity of others.

Never forget that mutual trust is the key to every great relationship. You must show trust in someone as much as you must earn their trust. When you trust someone, you help them become better and want to live up to their end of the relationship. Great relationships mean that both parties are unquestionably out for each other's best interest.

Chapter 25 | Be Mindful of your Inner Circle

Your friends exert strong gravity on you. It's really that simple. Your life becomes a reflection of the five or ten friends who you spend the 80% of your time with.

This leads full circle to specific ideas from earlier chapters. Every choice is your own and having any plan is better than no plan at all. There is little difference in where you land when looking for a job or when looking for friends. Many people "fall into" a job and many people "fall into friendships" but leaving your life to chance and hoping for the best rarely results in the best outcomes. If you want to rise above the average 70%, it's a darn good idea to find friends that will help you, not bring you back to average or even worse.

Although you might find making choices hard to do, step one is to recognize which of your friends are lifting you up versus which of your friends are dragging you down. Optimally, it would be brilliant to have a group of friends that make each other stronger, better, happier, and more resilient. Even though a few of your friends might be a lot of fun to be around, they might be the ones who invariably make sure that you stay out way too late, drink too much, miss meetings with hangovers, and in general, ensure that you will not advance easily. The difference between great success and just being average is in the daily details and you should not willingly risk keeping bad influences looming over your life for the short-term fun and distractions.

Above all else, you must pick friends who believe in your potential and encourage you to take smart risks. It is easy to give up too quickly. It is easy to listen to critics who invariably sound smart when they tell you to try something else.

Most people fall into one group, instead of constantly striving to branch out and make new connections. If you have not made a new uplifting-potential friend in a month or two, you are not trying hard enough. The world becomes a wondrous place when you consistently expand your network and your horizons, but you must take action: you must actively seek if you expect to find. It takes time and energy to find out if that new acquaintance is a great fit, but that investment is well worth it.

Looking outside your closest ten friends, you must also build a real network of people who not only know you by name, but know you well enough to introduce you to others as a good person to know. Something in human nature tends to make people specialize, and specialization closes doors of opportunity. Golfers usually golf, while racquetballers racquetball, and yoga people yoga. It is highly unusual to meet a Ferris Bueller who makes friends and connections across a vast number of unrelated groups. Be as Ferris as you can be, and you will be better off. If you can, become the connector that helps others connect and give that help freely. The more you help, the more positive things boomerang back to you over time. Remember people's names and write down reminders in your chosen permanotes system.

I recognized the benefits of an expanding personal network early on but, for some strange reason, limited my proactive efforts to just my workplace for years. It seemed natural but it completely limited my chances of finding interesting people in different walks of life. One day, I made a new friend at the gym — I had been going to that gym six days per week for years — and he opened my eyes to what I was missing. Dan made an effort and knew every regular there, hundreds of people, and it was such an interesting group once you got to know them. Becoming friends with Dan woke me up to how much more is possible if you simply look for opportunities and say something with a smile on your face.

The single most important decision that you are likely ever going to make is deciding who you will marry. That person will either help you reach your dreams and goals, will keep you on track, will recharge your emotional batteries when you need it, or not. Marry someone who has similar visions, values, and goals, someone who will grow and change with you, and your odds will improve a lot. Not only does divorce usually cost you half of everything financially, it also flat-out sucks. It takes most people years to get back on track and the seasons of life are an ever-present reality which ensures that time is scarce and valuable.

Lastly, diversity matters. Great teams always have complimentary skills and interests. Complimentary people do not fight for the same slot on the team. When a team all has people who are nearly alike, conflict tends to happen over time. Worse yet, everyone agrees too readily in the same direction, when what really helps is a healthy debate when the best ideas win.

Your closest friends' trajectory becomes your own. Their attitudes, optimism, and values will either help you or hurt you. Pick your friends mindfully and make an effort to surround yourself with friends that help your odds of escaping average, and on the other side of the coin, be sure and help them do the same. There is plenty of success to go around.

Chapter 26 | The 'Why' Matters Most, but Plan It Too

If you don't know where you want to go, you are unlikely to get there. Most people don't set serious life goals for themselves and then wander around hoping for the best. This does not work if you want to escape average.

Of the minority of people who do set goals, few achieve their goals in any reasonable timeframe, if ever. I have found that, too often:

- the goals are invariably vague,
- people set too many goals at once,
- people are not fully committed,
- they don't measure progress against their plan, because, frankly, there is rarely a written plan, and
- they listen too much to critics.

Vague goals are wishful daydreams. On the other hand, someone who writes down a specific goal, writes down exactly why the goal is important to her, creates a specific plan with milestones, puts specific tasks on a calendar, then takes massive, committed action, measures her progress, adapts, revises the plan, and overcomes setbacks, persists and focused on finishing stronger than she started, will make it happen.

Get specific. Here's how in just a few steps. If these steps below look like too much work to you, then the goal you are thinking about is not worth tackling this year. You are better off just narrowing it down to the goals that are worth planning well.

Answer these dozen key questions about this one goal:

(1) Description of the goal.
(one sentence)

(2) Why do you want to achieve this goal?
(one paragraph – be sure and include the benefits that you expect to receive from the achievement)

(3) How will you know that you have achieved the goal / how will you measure that it is really done?
(one or two sentences)

(4) By what specific date do you want to achieve this goal, and why is this date realistic?
(specific date, and some justification)

(5) What are the intermediary steps in high-level bullet form that are anticipated steps to achieve the goal?
(one line sentences, but leave 5 lines of space between each sentence)

(6) Please put dates and any other quantitative measurements you can on each one of the intermediate steps so that this goal will be on track to make the date specified in step 4.
(For example, if you are writing a book, the number of pages written by a date offers a great second milestone that can be measured, not just the date itself.)

(7) For each of the intermediary steps from step 5, list 2 – 10 tasks that are subcomponents of getting that intermediate step finished.
(one detailed line each)

(8) Whose help will you need help from to make these tasks happen?
(Write down not only the people or organization but also several bullets about the exact kind of help you will need from these people or organizations. Add dates to put these resources together.)

(9) Are there any skills that you need to develop to make these tasks happen?

(If there are skills that need developing, this is a subproject
that needs its own tasks and deadlines. Add these bullets to
your plan.)

(10) Is this goal in line with your overall direction / purpose in
your life?
(If it is not, it might not happen, because you will be fighting
against the current of your life's river every step of the way.)

(11) After jotting down this plan, are the time frames and
milestone dates achievable?
(It's ok to be aggressive but if the plan is completely
unreasonable, you will find that you give up soon after you
get started. You must make it mission possible, not mission
impossible. If the milestones look way out of logical
possibility, go back and adjust the dates and final
achievement target.)

(12) What are the first 5 tasks? Put them down on your near-
term list with deadlines.
(Get started on time, since getting started is the key to getting
motivated. It is much harder to push a car from a standstill
into motion. Once rolling, it takes less power to keep it rolling
forward.)

Right about now, you might be thinking holy moly, that's a lot to
figure out. Yes, it is, but it helps weed out weak goals from worthy
ones, and it helps you get off to a great start.

There are few things more important than knowing what you truly
want. Begin with the end in mind. Nothing helps as much as step
#2 — the "why". When the "why" is strong enough, people have
little problem figuring out the "what" and the "how" and the
"time" and the "resources" to get to the finish line on any project.

Planning, in general, is the best way to live if you want to achieve
great things.

Imagine being a professional football coach, getting the team on the plane, and simply showing up for the Superbowl without a game plan and offensive and defensive plays to run? Or imagine what would happen if you decided to build yourself a new mansion without having an architect draw up blueprints. Or imagine being a general facing an enemy platoon on a bloody battlefield and not having a plan to coordinate your own troops? Or imagine having a big wedding without any lists for anyone involved. No endeavor goes as well as it should without careful planning.

Always have a Plan A and a Plan B if Plan A falters, even in small matters. Take the time to plan — always in writing — for the meeting with a client. It helps to have a few bullet points for a call with your boss. As complexity grows, planning needs to take centerstage.

The truth is most people don't take the time to plan. Most simply react. If you anticipate what might happen, you can design what you will do in a stressful moment when things go south. Even when you don't anticipate well and something does surprise you, you can make plans for how to buy yourself some time and space to think. Planning for all scenarios is a valuable exercise.

Ultimately, success has a lot to do with making the right decisions at the right point in time. You are in essence, trying to play chess, thinking five or ten moves ahead, instead of playing checkers. Planning helps you prepare in advance and make better decisions more consistently.

When you work through your Plan B, you become more flexible and resilient. Plan B helps you think in terms of 'not yet', what did I learn, and how will I adapt and overcome. If you pivot from Plan A to Plan B, that is the perfect time to think up Plan C, just in case your Plan B is flawed and fails to make progress.

Lastly, plan far ahead. Anticipate what you will do next, and next after that, after you succeed on the current number one priority mission. Staying ahead will help you connect the dots and make progress all the much faster.

If a goal is important enough to do it, to go for it, always create a written plan with specifics. There are entire books written about goals but this simple formula, above, is most of what you need.

Chapter 27 | Defeating the Stress Hairball

People, especially high achievers, beat themselves up mentally, far more often than they realize. Inside one's own head, there can be a frequent struggle between forces like "I'm pretty awesome and I can do this..." versus "Why have I failed up to this point..."; "Why is my work not perfect..."; and "Why did I miss the deadline...".

A great habit is to burn into your mind's OS is to adopt a simple phrase into your thinking whenever you don't quite accomplish exactly what you planned. When your boss asks you a question like "Did you sell the Devlin Macgregor account..." or if your parents ask you "Did you get a promotion..." or if your sister asks you "Do you have a girlfriend...", always answer with *"not yet."*

Admitting 'not yet' to yourself is important — you not only buy yourself time to adapt and overcome, but you also reduce the effect of self-sabotaging stress. You might be thinking 'not yet' is just an excuse but in truth, in most cases, it is not. A lame excuse is when you cover up for your attempts by claiming that you did everything that you could. 'Not yet' is admitting the reality that great things often take more time than your hoped and great tenacity and perseverance is needed to get to the finish line.

Many people quit when they run into an obstacle. These two words separate a failure from a setback to learn lessons from. Take a breath and then whisper "not yet" to yourself. There is great wisdom in failing fast, failing often, failing forward. You must adapt and overcome.

How often have we heard 'I tried everything to make it happen, but nothing worked'? How often have you said this yourself? Was this statement ever true?

The reality is that nearly everyone gives up after trying just one or two ways attempted. Three distinctly different attempts are quite rare, reserved for only the most important of endeavors. People shoot themselves in the foot when they announce that they "have tried everything" because nothing can be farther from the truth. When you make announcements, they become your own limiting belief. Sadly, a lot of people get mentally stuck, simply trying the same methods, over and over, expecting different results but not getting them.

I see few examples of anyone trying multiple paths and methods. This is true for the math teacher trying to get her lesson embraced by her student, or the student who tries to memorize the key elements needed for the upcoming exam. This is true for the coach trying to help his team win, the manager striving to make his sales team hit the forecasted numbers, the entrepreneur trying to win customers for her start-up, and it's true for millions of people hoping to improve their physical fitness. Most everyone tries only one or two ways — sometimes for months and years — and then gives up.

So how do the extraordinary few actually succeed?

Getting started as soon as possible is truly step one. Waiting for all the lights to turn green before driving across town is futile — yet many wait for the perfect moment and fail to get out of the starting gate. The often-forgotten reality is that getting started comes before getting motivated. Many believe it is the other way around.

What truly matters most — in the long-run — is whole-hearted, stake your life on it, commitment. Jumping into the deep end with both feet makes up for any shortcomings that you have in raw talent. All of us have gaps in talent. Your commitment level is the single most important factor that changes how many distinct ways you will try to overcome a challenge. If you decide that "I **must** succeed at _________ " instead of "I want to succeed at _________ ", you will find that your success percentages will dramatically improve.

A great quote to memorize came from Hall of Fame football coach, Vince Lombardi: *"Winning means you are willing to go longer, work harder, and give more than anyone else."*

Imagine two people, Nick and Mike, who both hope to invent the next big thing. Nick, in his own mind's eye, simply says "I want to" and so, he will work on his project whenever time allows, after he does his day job, hangs with his family, works out at the gym, sees his friends, checks his social media, watches the ball game, and catches up on the news. Mike, on the other hand, commits whole-heartedly and says "I must" — and this one little difference makes all the difference. He etches out hours, each and every week without fail, when he runs into an obstacle he utters "not yet" as he pivots, adapts, and overcomes, he gets to the finish line of the project, succeeding with persistence and tenacity. It is rarely about talent alone. Success is invariably about your commitment. Commitment is the seed of will power. Only the committed are relentless in the pursuit.

Embrace the power of 'not yet' to reduce your natural overachiever stress. Stress mostly comes from feeling lack of control, going over possible futures, lists and unknowns non-stop, and comparing yourself to others. Stress drops off when you realize it is taking longer than planned (not yet), you "always do your best daily, with what you actually have to work with", and that best should include trying many different things to adapt and overcome.

Outside of the internal 'top achiever' stress, it is important to develop stress deflection Teflon, overall. People are mostly completely and utterly wrong in their thinking about stress. They believe stress is an external thing, an invisible fog that rolls in and surrounds you, to the point that you feel and suffer from the stress. In truth, stress comes from our own focus and beliefs, it comes from inside of us, and it becomes real to us because we make it real, in our own minds.

I had moments where stress really impacted my physical health, and thankfully, I learned important lessons without having a coronary incident. I was juggling way too many balls in the air at work, investments had all turned for the worse and I owned a lot of long-term stock options so time was working against me, and I simply had overcommitted on many fronts, forgetting that priority is the right word to use in life, not priorities. I started having frequent visual migraines and, not knowing what they were, wound up in a doctor's office as he ordered an MRI of my head to check for brain cancer. Holy sh*t! I have never fainted in my life, but that one day, I turned white as a sheet and came rather close as the nurse ran to get some ice.

Luckily the MRI simply showed the lasting remnants of the migraines and nothing else, and I learned that stress was mostly self-created. Sure, there are outside influences that can be triggers, but your perspectives of those influences, how you think about those outside events, changes everything. From that day forward, I have become far more conscious of intentionally taking a Zen approach, committing to get up each morning and simply do my very best, understanding that no matter the outcome, I can take comfort that I did my best, and that my best is enough.

Within weeks, I went from experiencing a visual migraine every few days to not having one for a year or more. I had reprogrammed my thinking in just a few hours. The outside problems had not changed but my perspective had: *Life is 10% what happens to you and 90% how you think about it and react to it.* As a nice little added benefit, I no longer feel stress in traffic for I now see it as the external trigger that it really is, mostly something I can't control.

Most people mistakenly feel that they are more in control of a lot of aspects of their life than they really are. You must understand your personal circle of control clearly and accurately. Those who learn to focus and think about the aspects of life that they can, truly control, while leaving the things that they can't to God, or the

Force, or fate, or chance (depending on your views) live a life of far less stress and greater happiness.

When we think about potential scenarios in the future, or we think about past events, we are adding to our stress, because stress is completely and undeniably linked to the sphere we can't control. We cannot control how the future plays out, nor can we change the past. We can only affect the present, and even in the here and now, only a subset can be controlled there.

Much of life is like the stock market. What happened to a stock in the past is not indicative of what will happen to that stock's price tomorrow, or next month, or next year. Hundreds if not thousands of aspects come into play, which is why billions of dollars of computer systems and artificial intelligence still can't reliably predict the future.

Once you realize how small your circle of control is and accept the rest of the universe as stuff that you won't worry about until it actually enters your circle of control, you are well on your way to 90% stress deflection.

At the same time, it is important to accurately understand your influence, not just your control, on your work, your workplace, your family, and your broader social circles. When you accurately understand what you can influence, you become happier. You must feel that you can influence things for the better to feel good about your life overall. Otherwise, you are just a pinball in the pinball machine, bouncing off paddles and bumpers until the game is over. If you are in a job where you have zero control, zero impact, and zero influence, take control back and go find a better slot elsewhere: you will be happier in the long run. Don't quit first – it's easier to get a new job while still working on the current job – but start interviewing asap.

No one ever gets to 100% stress-deflection if he or she lives in the normal world of hustling for a living and for advancement. This is because we must make daily decisions, and those decisions are usually made by estimating what will happen in the near future, and of course, future results are out of our circle of control. This comes full circle to how awesome it would be to have the superpower of always making the best decision possible. As discussed earlier, you can choose to really think through decisions, to research, to consult advisors and mentors, or live life on a comes-what-may basis, but the top successful folks all strive for making the best decision possible.

A truly magic moment comes when you realize that the one thing that you can 100% control is the quality of your effort and thinking each day. You can't control who wins the game today, but you can control the quality of your effort. Sleep well if you did your absolute best. I might lose today, but that's ok, if I gave it my best. I can control the quality of my efforts tomorrow. I can learn, adapt, and know that I will not lose my enthusiasm, I will not lose my will, and I will get up and do my best tomorrow. That is the moment, if you can make this "I will always give it my best" a daily habitual part of your mental operating system, that you become a top 1%'er in stress avoidance, which leads to greater happiness, health, and success overall.

I like to think of life like a soccer game and I'm playing center midfielder and at times, player coach. Life is a team sport, and you never win every game. My midfielder job is well defined with some room for creativity, but it takes the entire team to win. The defense, the goalkeeper, the wingers, the striker all have a role to play as well, as does the opposing team, the refs, and the fans. Stick to what you can do, while helping and influencing all those around you to do their best and worry a lot less about the score.

Chapter 28 | Health is Usually not Accidental

Imagine that the day you turned 20, you got the one and only car you could own for the rest of your life. How would you care for your car? Carefully, right? You would not miss maintenance intervals. You probably would not race it or leave pizza boxes on the leather seats. If you only got one car in life, you would baby it.

All of us only get one mind and one body in life, but too often, many people inhale a huge bag of Cool Ranch Doritos while sitting on the couch bingeing on Netflix. People stay out until 3 am, pound shots and bottles of wine, and wake up with raging hangovers. You skip the sunblock when you head down to the pool to make sure you get a quick start on your tan, future skin cancer not a worry. You haven't read a great book this year, but you know exactly what's happened to Taylor Swift and the outlook for Dak Prescott's latest injury.

Health is mostly not an accident, although differences in genetics play a part. The science is mostly obvious: if you don't dedicate time and effort to physical fitness, your foundation of health will crumble. To be a fit 55-year-old, you must invest the time when you are 45. Physical fitness isn't hard with some clean living, eating quality foods in moderation, spending half your fitness time on aerobic, sweaty exercise, and the other half your time strengthening and toning your muscles. Eating far too much, drinking a lot of alcohol, smoking, vaping, experimenting with drugs all destroy your health, given enough time and volume. Big tobacco would never have become a billion-dollar industry if tobacco killed people fast, but killing people slowly works when people are short-term in their thinking.

Nothing will crash your life faster, or hurt your family more, than the demise of your health.

It has nothing to do with how smart you are. A few years ago, I played a lot of racquetball at the gym. One of the regulars was a

PhD researcher for a large pharma manufacturer. Glenn was smart as a tack, an entertaining guy, and a darn good player considering that he was significantly overweight and clearly trying to slim down. Unfortunately, Glenn left his family and this world at 47, when he suffered a massive stroke right in the middle of a game. I had never seen a massive stroke firsthand. It was quite a wakeup call for those of us that witnessed it. There are no guarantees but don't let yourself deteriorate since making a comeback is not guaranteed — start with good health habits now.

If you want to escape average and strive for outlier success, mental fitness is just as important. You must stay curious and become a lifelong student and thinker. Just like with food, good mental input yields better ideas while garbage input yields little of value. Read at least one good book each month — for life. Find friends who are great to debate with. Watch quality video, not just mindless entertainment — TED.com videos and Masterclass.com classes are great examples. Journal your thoughts as writing helps you remember longer-term and knit fresh ideas together. Take a class. The list goes on.

A large portion of the success formula in the real-world has to do with emotional and social intelligence. Remembering people's names, remembering small details is perhaps the greatest difference between EQ / SQ success or failure. If you can't remember that Jim was excited about his opportunity to go to the Masters golf tournament in Augusta, how would you rekindle your connection with him the next time you see him months later?

It turns out that there are proven memory techniques that, when learned and habitualized, can help you run circles around average people in terms of remembering names and details. Back in the days of Plato, Socrates, and Aristotle, the Greeks gave speech after speech without notes. When humans didn't rely on the ink pen and PowerPoint, we developed great, effective techniques to remember what we wanted to remember, in the order we wanted to remember it. These methods were mostly lost and forgotten as we became more modern, but the techniques are generally understood, practiced, documented, and in truth, not especially difficult to learn.

Imagine meeting twenty-five new people when you arrive at an art gallery for an artist's new showing. Wine is flowing, and there are plenty of distractions. The average person might remember one or two new names, if any. Yet there are memory masters who have perfected the techniques to be able to meet a hundred people in a row and remember each person's name hours later. The core principle is that if you can think of a vivid visual reminder when a person introduces herself to you, the act of visualization helps put her name in long term memory and out of short-term working memory.

For example, I met a new guy at the gym named Aaron who looked nothing like an "Aaron" to me. I decided to visualize quarterback Aaron Rogers in his Green Bay Packers uniform for just a few seconds while talking with gym-Aaron. It was nothing but a simple visualization habit that can be easily learned and habitualized. Even now, years later, I not only remember Aaron's name but also what he looked like. The following week, I met a guy named Barrett, visualized a barrel, and instantly remembered his name for years. The simplicity of the technique is amazing. All it takes a bit of practice and reprogramming your mental habits.

These techniques are not hard to learn, but can really help you improve your memory skills, no matter if you want to use them to remember names, or the points of a presentation that you are planning to give or lists that you want to remember for school. For a few videos illustrating the techniques used by memory contest competitors, visit escavg.com/memory — it really is fascinating and will help you with your memory, one of the keys to mental fitness.

The last component to superior health is finding a spiritual connection. For some, it is God and religion while for others it might be mindfulness and meditation. It will come if you make an effort, if you find connection and peace, if you become more aware of your surroundings and the wonder we enjoy on Earth.

A final thought about health and fitness: It is important to realize that while a lot of health is in your control, things sometimes happen that change things dramatically. For example, a car accident or the onset of a disease has suddenly ruined many a person's health or capabilities. If life throws you a health curveball, realize that it is 100% up to you to play the cards that you have been dealt, to make the best of it. It won't be easy, but plenty of people have come back to become the best that they can be, given new limitations. If someone else has been able to do it, so can you. You can if you think you can.

In my own life, blowing out the anterior cruciate ligament (ACL) in my left knee probably saved my fitness. I then made the wrong choice and waited over a year before facing the situation and having the reconstruction. My choice to delay the inevitable led to a significant degradation of my leg because the nature of human anatomy is that you have to use it, or you will lose it. Muscles atrophy when not used. In my case, I started relying on my right leg for 90% of strength and the left leg as mostly just an assistant for balance, which leads to one weak and skinny leg. After the knee surgery, the only path back is to go to the gym and put in the work, if you ever expect to be playing sports well again. While at the gym, I decided that I might as well do complete workouts and now, twenty years later, I rarely miss more than one day a week from my efforts to staying fit.

Invest time recharging yourself. Many don't really take off when they are off work. No one ever says that they wished that they had spent more time at the office when they are dying. If you take care of your mind and your body like it's the only one you will have, you are far more likely to play a little soccer or go ride bicycles with your grandkids when you are seventy-five.

There are two ways to lead. Leadership through position and title is the obvious one, limited to just a minority, but leadership through peer influence and the power of your ideas is available to anyone who takes the initiative, builds relationships, and paints a compelling vision. When you are young, you often don't realize how much room there is to lead without having the organizational title and blessing. It takes some time to get your feet on the ground, to understand the pecking order and build your allies, but you should not wait to take the lead until after you get promoted into a management role.

Great leadership starts with innovation and ideas. Not every idea will be a winner just like not every song goes platinum: Busy artists with lots of songs get to the Rock and Roll Hall of Fame, not the one hit wonders. Great leadership requires lots of ideas, collaboration on ideas, the flexibility to pivot when needed, and the will power to push forward when you are on the right track. Great leaders "sell" others on their ideas, as opposed to simply smashing people over the head with them.

The test of leadership is whether you have influence to the point of another person taking action. If people listen to you, say you are on the right track, but do not act, you may think you are leading them but in truth, your efforts are falling short. This is a good time to simply say "not yet" and adjust your methods, do things a bit differently, and see if you become more effective.

What separates good leaders from great leaders is inspiring others to accomplish more than they thought they could. Great leaders sell their vision and ideas, inspire the need for change and urgency, and gain disciples. Poor leaders may have the organizational authority but spend their days issuing top-down commands, micromanaging people until they run them off or extinguish their enthusiasm. A simple but lasting leadership strategy is to lead by example, not command.

True leadership comes from a state-of-mind that looks for innovative solutions to problems, combined with credibility that is earned through competence, integrity, vision, decisiveness, and the ability to communicate effectively.

While a lot of things must come together to create the magic of "earned" leadership, two of the most important are initiative and clarity.

Initiative is a great differentiator between a leader and a follower. Keep a log of new things that you initiate. Log initiative that you see taken by others in your network. Ink will open your eyes and help you see how rare initiative is and highlight the opportunity that you have to lead.

Clarity matters, yet it is often missing. Colin Powell observed that "Great leaders are almost always great simplifiers, who can cut through argument, debate and doubt to offer a solution everybody can understand."

Do you want to lead and grow as a leader? Don't wait until someone "appoints you" as a leader. Start today by taking some initiative and communicate your vision clearly and concisely. Then, evaluate your effectiveness. Does your initiative cause change? Keep a log and study what happens. Everything takes practice yet so few actually practice, especially in the workplace. Writing it down will keep you honest with yourself, keep your momentum, and help you learn and improve.

I made some painful mistakes around leadership, especially the leadership of appointed managers, in my twenties and thirties. I struggled with leaders who said, *"do it this way, do it now, because I said so."* I wanted to debate the logic, to be sold and persuaded, not told. I wasn't wise then, reacting by transforming into the suit wearing version of a little kid, asking "why, why, why" in multiple ways and debating the value of the commanded directive. That tactic does not make you any manager's favorite and erodes your influence quickly. Over time, I have learned that you must understand the manager's personality well and seed ideas much earlier in the process, usually in a one-on-one setting, so that he assimilates the ideas, makes the ideas his own, and makes it part of his plan and eventual command from on high. You can always have influence, but you must play your cards well, with good timing. No manager likes a subordinate who questions his judgement, especially if others are present. I have also learned that managers from different countries and cultures have dramatically different expectations of feedback and debate from subordinates. This sounds so simple to understand now, but in the heat of the moment, I have repeated this mistake numerous times.

Effective persuasion and taking initiative are aspects that all of us must strive to master. While these aspects are front and center job requirements of sales professionals, we are all selling when we try to convince our work colleagues, customers, friends, or family members to agree with our point of view and to ultimately take action. Great persuasion starts by understanding the other's perspective and finding common ground, then finding a path to a win/win scenario. Often, the best way to persuade someone to take action in the way that you hope is to first help define and clarify the problem so that your vision, your idea becomes the logical best path for a solution. Ultimately, people act for their own reasons, not yours, so the most effective of influencers are the ones who help people find those reasons.

It is crucial to take the initiative and learn to be a strong influence on your colleagues and your management. Just remember that you must play the role of a good troop as well, and, if your appointed leader is going in the wrong direction, you will have to make some subtle, deft moves with good timing to get him to change the direction, not oppose him in an obvious, win/lose scenario, in a public forum. Don't repeat the mistake that I took nearly ten years to learn. Often, the right way might be to build a consortium or to go at it through a person who is the right-hand consigliere of the manager. There are many nuances to leadership and there is always more to learn. Effective persuasion requires adjusting your approach to fit the person you hope to influence.

Chapter 30 | Don't Swim Upstream

Do you have a goal of being well off financially by the time you are 50 or 55? It's really not that hard, if you have self-discipline. Unfailingly save and invest 10% of what you earn, avoid taking on debt for stuff that loses value over time, and have patience to let compounding gains work their magic. Warren Buffet didn't get mega-rich overnight. In fact, Warren has made most of his money after the age of 60. Time is an important factor.

By investing capital in assets that appreciate, you take advantage of the system that most free democracies are founded on. Unfortunately, most people don't avoid debt, especially insidious consumer debt. When you borrow money to purchase a home, there is a good chance that the home will be an asset that appreciates over time. If you purchased in the right neighborhood, there is a chance that the appreciation will be greater than the hard expenses you paid in interest, property taxes, maintenance, and improvement. Most consumer debt, on the other hand, is used to buy more stuff, stuff that then vaporizes your money. Cars lose half their value in the first three years after leaving the dealership. Clothes, purses, shoes, sporting equipment, furniture, and computers all lose most of their value instantly and become worthless donations a few years later. Paying interest expense for stuff that will never appreciate, just to possess it before you can afford it, nukes your long-term financial outlook. Debt makes everything cost more.

Capitalism is the best system for economic prosperity the world has ever seen up to this point. Capitalism has made America, a country with only 5% of the humans on this planet, an absolute superpower. But make no mistake that there are relentless forces at play. Capitalism rewards capitalists more than it rewards workers, it rewards the people who own the businesses, either directly or through shares of publicly traded companies. It also fuels the system which encourages consumers to spend on trivial items and go into greater debt.

Let me start with the bottom line. When you live within a system, it pays to play the game in the way the game is favored, if you want to escape average and become an above average success. You must go with the flow, not swim upstream. Odds always favor the owners of a casino, not the people playing roulette and blackjack.

Starting a business is raw unbridled capitalism, which comes with the potential for greater success or greater failure. There is invariably risk that all you have invested in your venture could vaporize, but with that risk comes the potential for reward.

Employment, on the other hand, is like bunting to get on base versus swinging mightily for a home run. How much you make as an employee is governed by the uniqueness of your value-add to the company, and by the supply and demand of others like you. It is much better to be a rare employee with rare, specialized skills that solves expensive problems than it is to be one of the herd. A diligent accountant will never make more than a proven, rainmaking salesperson who brings in millions in new business, and has proven herself in multiple territories and situations.

Here is the first most reality of capitalism: Capitalism rewards the successful business owner far more than the successful employee, because the owner is rewarded for the risk that she took in addition to the effort that she put in.

Don't swim upstream, fighting the capitalistic system. You must own shares of successful, growing businesses even if you never start your own company. The great news is that you can participate in capitalism, anyone can participate as a capitalist, via stock and bond ownership. The stock market is an incredible leveler of opportunity. Anyone can save up capital and invest it in successful, growing companies. Of course, it is best to buy shares of companies at a fair price, which takes a bit of understanding of value. Warren Buffett didn't buck the system; rather, he leveraged ownership to become one of richest people on Earth.

I would recommend reading just three books to start so that you get your feet on the ground with investing in stocks. Visit escavg.com/threebooks for a one-page summary and the links.

The magic of compounding investment gains works like a charm, if you have a long enough runway. Compounding won't do much for a person who starts saving just ten years before retirement, but thirty years works wonders. The one thing that I really did right financially — the one thing that made a huge difference throughout my life — was to start early, get ahead, and stay ahead on the savings and investment front. Long before I got married, long before I had kids, I started saving and investing, tracking my investments, striving to find new ideas, and developing a formula for success. From the time I was 23 until I was 33, I saved more than 20% of what I earned and mostly invested it in stocks of fairly priced, fast-growing companies.

I did learn some important lessons from painful mistakes — for example, if something sounds too good to be true, it is always too good to be true. At 22, I lost most of my early savings on trading soybeans and silver. The brokers are adept at convincing you that they have inside knowledge. They hope you win for a while which means you add more capital to your early bets, and trade more often. It's only a matter of time until you lose. What the heck did I know about soybeans? You must make your own investment decisions, know and write down why you believe a stock is a good investment at a fair price, and avoid external pressure from sell side "professionals" who benefit from your activity. Hot tips are bullsh*t.

Getting ahead on saving and investing is brilliant, because you will then have money to survive rainy days. Compounding means that your money grows over time, with your gains fueling more gains in the future. Murphy's Law remains as prevalent as ever. If you have no savings, it only takes something small to put you into the tailspin of debt.

I believe, based on my own experience and contrary to the incantations and marketing of Wall Street, that outperforming the averages is quite possible for any investor. If you can outperform the S&P 500 by an average of just 2% over thirty years, your end balance will be dramatically greater and well worth the time and effort.

Outside of investing your financial capital, assuming that you are participating in capitalism as an employee, you must build up your expertise, adding increasingly unique value to your company. You must be on a never-ending quest to become better, to become harder and harder to replace, to add more value per day than almost anyone else. This will move you up the pay scale over time, although there are different limits on your specific career — a Registered Nurse has a different opportunity scope than a Licensed Realtor than an I.T. Enterprise Architect. Achieving true expertise often takes thousands of hours of work and practice while stretching yourself, so be sure that the area you are working in will lead to where you want to go.

It is difficult to rise to the top of an organization. There are lots of highly competent competitors all vying for the few slots that only open rarely. Some will have better connections and mentors than others, so it is not just smarts and ability. But the opportunity to own shares of a successful business are open to all. Your chance to become a rare expert who gets paid exceedingly well is open to all as well. Play the game of capitalism well with your eyes wide open, instead of sitting in a park holding up a sign and protesting the top one percent. Capitalism has made America the one true superpower and therefore, common sense says that it is unlikely to change in this lifetime.

You might think that capitalism and democracy isn't fair; after all, many a confused but well-intentioned professor has told you how awesome it is in Sweden or Denmark with healthcare and education for all. Socialism is worse than capitalism for anyone with ambition, anyone who loves the fairness of a meritocracy, because socialism systematically reduces a person's hustle and for that matter, the hustle of an entire nation. Communism offers socialism but in a setting where the authoritative government owns most enterprises, and is pretty much, a completely failed economic experiment. But here's the wakeup call — chances are that changing the system you live within is outside your personal circle of control. If you happen to live in Sweden, go with the flow and play the Swedish 'game' the best that you can.

Don't swim against the current. If you live in a free, capitalistic society, play the game capitalism well. You must become an owner, a capitalist, to gain a favorable advantage.

One last lesson that I have learned that is well worth mentioning. If you work for a large company, there will be a company-specific system and culture in place there. While being a maverick might differentiate you and get you noticed, it is important to transition to thriving within the system, not outside the system. It doesn't usually pay to swim upstream forever at your company as you will tire. Find ways to be noticed, to be special, to add unique value, but then take advantage of the existing gears and work with the system, not against it.

Chapter 31 | Swinging for the Fence

In the last chapter, we discussed the idea that you have a better chance of escaping average, at least financially, by playing the game of capitalism well when you live and work in a capitalist society or country.

Most people do not start their own company, but if you have the desire and the goal, starting your own company is playing the game of capitalism to its fullest, it is swinging with all your might to hit a financial home run over the left-field fence.

I started my own smartphone software company in 2006, focused on the BlackBerry. We had a wild seven-year run, on a roller coaster with great ups and great downs as well. There were lots of failures and obstacles, we tried lots of ideas and pricing models, and I learned many incredible lessons — it would take a small book to share them all — maybe I'll write that one in the future.

The good news is that you don't have to wait for my future book. If you are interested, I would highly recommend taking in Sara Blakeney's full class on Masterclass.com. Sara founded Spanx on a meager $5,000 shoestring, navigated the maze, kept her full ownership, and, after a lot of hard work and tenacity, became a billionaire. As I watched her entertaining class about the real-world, I found that there were an amazing number of similarities with her experience, with her thinking, and with what she did, compared to what we did during our venture. She obviously did it better, didn't get torpedoed like we did, and made it through the gauntlet in far better shape, hitting that home run over the fence. If you want to be an entrepreneur, invest your time and watch Sara's masterclass.

After these lessons learned, I would like to share how I evaluate new ventures today. I think this short list will help you if you have the desire to swing for the fence.

Take a couple of sheets on paper, and answer these questions, then use it as a starting point to discuss your answers with three or more wise mentors:

Evaluating a New Idea for a Business Venture:

1. What is the main problem you are going to solve? Is this a problem that people accurately see and understand is a problem?

2. Are people actively looking for a solution to the problem? If they are, how many people are searching for a solution each day? Are there unique yet obvious keywords that will be used when performing the search? If yes, how expensive will it be to appear in the search results on Google? Will it be easy or hard to target ads to the right audience on Facebook, Instagram, and other social media?

3. Are you trying to create a new market where there is no market today? If yes, be aware that it is infinitely harder to create a new market than to fit in a market where transactions are already flowing.

4. How easy is it to understand? Can the problem be articulated 30 seconds or less? Can your solution be articulated in 30 seconds or less? Can your differentiation be clearly shown in 30 seconds or less? Is this problem-solution-differentiation equation memorable and visually stimulating or conceptual and ho-hum. We live in a world of constant, digital media amplified noise. Clarity matters.

5. Is solving the problem financially valuable? If a problem is not painful, it is hard for prospects to spend ongoing dollars.

6. Does your solution have a daily-use or weekly-use factor to it? One time use items are much harder in terms of producing customer loyalty and a steady stream of income.

7. Is it newsworthy? PR builds brands, while advertising only maintains brands. Does the solution have enough pizzaz to make it into newspaper articles?

8. Does the solution have what it takes to become word-of-mouth viral? People don't spread the word without a reason. Does your solution make them look smart, aware, and helpful?

9. Is the solution or product easy enough for you to create it? What will it take to be 10+% better than competitors?

10. What is the technology expertise needed to pull this off? The trickier, the harder to find resources, the more care and feeding, the longer it takes to develop, the harder for the customer to adopt it into daily / weekly use.

11. Who are the competitors? What is their position versus yours? What are the unique differentiators between each possible solution a customer would purchase?

12. How much do competitors matter? It is hard to rise above in a market that is crowded already. A perfect example is creating a new iOS app in an area where the natural search keywords have hundreds of listings.

13. Can demand be measured before plunging in? How much will it cost to get to a point where you are testing the viability of the product or solution? How much will it cost until you have tested the market?

14. Is it an island / silo solution or does it lead to other places?

15. How much on-going support will it require?

This list is not comprehensive, but I believe it offers a lot of value, and lets you get your thoughts on paper as you engage with your hopefully optimistic, can-do group of mentors.

Sara made one point that I think is super-important. Don't tell everybody what you are doing too early in the process or you will get hit with a ton of "this will never work" or "there is no way you will pull it off" criticism. Timing matters.

Chapter 32 | What Gets Measured Gets Improved

Why do most successful companies improve their book value, and often their market capitalization, year in and year out? There are a great number of reasons but one that really stands out is that they carefully measure their progress. Using Costco as an example, the company measures sales per store location, sales as compared to the previous month and quarter, sales as compared to the same quarter last year, labor costs, marketing costs, capital investment and more. Headquarters slices and dices the numbers, and then fine-tunes and corrects its course to optimize the expenses, sales, and profit contributions.

When you invest in Costco stock, you are investing in a group of professionals who will measure their own business and then do what it takes to get the main goal accomplished, namely grow the business in a profitable way such that your shares will grow over time as well.

How many people measure themselves — accurately, consistently, relentlessly — to achieve their goals? Most average people do not. What if you made the choice to measure your net worth every month or every three months starting when you are twenty-two years old? Would you improve your focus on net worth? Would you save and invest more? Would you avoid taking on debt at a whim?

Peter Drucker, perhaps the greatest thinker in recent times when it comes to the modern corporation, observed that "*What gets measured, gets improved.*" He was right.

While we all can appreciate how measuring investments and expenditures can help you focus on progress with your net worth, this applies to many of the habits found in [ESC][AVG].

A few years ago, I fell into the nasty habit of complaining too often. I believe the bad habit started with traffic — traffic is easy to complain about — but the bad habit then started to erode my daily positive attitude, impacting a couple of hours of each day. Complaints tend to spread to other arenas, so I decided to start measuring just to improve my consciousness.

I downloaded an iPhone tallying app and decided to click every time I caught myself complaining. The results were amazing. Within three weeks, I had stopped all complaints without much effort.

It is easy to see how measurement helps in normal life. If you start writing down your calories, before you start the meal, you will eat less, snack less, and eat better. If you start writing down the days that you do aerobic exercise on a highly visible calendar, you will work out more often. If you start measuring how often your daughter tries to score and shoots "on goal" in soccer, she will soon enough start shooting more often. If you take the effort to write down every time you catch yourself complaining, you will soon complain less. It works everywhere. If you want change, find a good way to measure it, a way that contributes to better daily decision making.

If you want to add a good new habit or get rid of a bad one, measure it. It is not about herculean effort and will power. Success starts with well-designed measurement which leads to awareness which leads to focus which leads to habit change.

Do you want to become more creative? Start by measuring the number of diverse books that you read. Do you want to become a more interesting conversationalist? Maybe measure the number of TED.com videos you watch. Don't forget to take a few notes in your permanotes on either of these ideas so that you can review them and remember them years later.

Want to lose weight? Weight watchers built their entire business on measuring in such a way that helps people substitute veggies for fried proteins. Download a calorie counting app and you will be amazed at your progress.

Do you want to improve your skills at work? Start measuring your skills improvement over time.

Do you want to improve your financial net worth? Start by measuring your progress each month and you will. If you find that you are not making progress, your measurements might be a bit too long term. People need measurements that matter in the here and now. If you find yourself not making progress, reconsider and fine-tune your measures. If you are not saving money on a monthly basis, maybe a highly visible glass jar and twenty bucks a day in cash, with a deposit to your investment account once a month, would change your results.

Chapter 33 | Surfing the Banzai Pipeline

Life is more like surfing than it is like water skiing, yet most people seem to mentally prepare themselves for water skiing. When water skiing, the driver of the boat looks for calm water and if he is good, drives a laser straight line at a constant speed, while the skier works on his skill at slaloming back and forth across the wake. The skier can adjust the speed of the boat with a simple thumbs up or thumb down indication to the driver and he can also decide how hard he will push himself in each carving change of direction and angle of attack across the wake.

Surfing on the other hand is a truly dynamic environment. Waves come rolling in and as they approach the shallows of the reef, they rise majestically out of the water. The surfer must notice the subtle differences as each wave approaches, pick the wave she feels is best suited for a great ride, embrace the moment, ride the swell like her life depends on it, and hopefully, avoid getting smashed onto the shallow jagged rocks and reef so close below. The reef below can have caverns that capture air and water for brief spells, adding random danger. The wind adds more energy and unpredictability. Places such as the renown Banzai Pipeline on Oahu's north shore have claimed plenty of experienced surfer lives over the years. The glory of the ride doesn't last long, and then she paddles her way back, against the waves, to get in position for another wonderful, exhilarating moment in the sun.

Life offers us waves over a shallow reef, but most people prepare for the predictability of the Mastercraft ski boat and calm, glassy water. Throughout your life, you will have waves even if you remain with one company, but most people will change between beaches, point breaks, and reef breaks many times over the years. The one true constant in life is change, as life is unfailingly dynamic, changing at unexpected times like a wave that closes out, and crashes down on the surfer unexpectedly.

Through [ESC][AVG], specific disciplines exist to help with your flexibility and adaptability. It is crucial, if you want to rise above average, that you decide to surf the waves of change, to seek the new wave of change, to embrace change enthusiastically, spot subtle hints of change, to be flexible in your thinking and approach, to adapt to changing situations, and be ready and fully committed to jump on a change. Most people see change as a threat yet the select few, the ones that have made the decision to love change, see change as a likely opportunity for things to improve.

The surfer must decide to be a surfer. While it pays to have a plan, don't get stuck planning forever. Analysis paralysis will not help you catch the next great wave. Overthinking is a huge problem for many people. People sit around feeling sorry for themselves when they perceive not-fair moments happen and the wave crashes them onto the shallow reef. The most successful people are often the Action Jacksons of the world (old movie title if you are wondering), the ones who spring into massive decisive action without second guessing themselves.

A perfect example is the dreaded corporate layoff or reorganization. Companies trigger these when the numbers turn ugly, or when new leaders take over, or when old leaders have a new plan, or when consultants create a new plan, and a lot of good people get ejected and displaced during these indiscriminate times. Many people over-analyze the situation, get angry at the world and the unfairness of it all, and after a long time, finally show up for some interviews, often with the look of defeat etched on their faces. The average person only looks at job opportunities that seem like the job that he just had. A person destined for the top 10%, on the other hand, goes with the flow. Just a couple of days after the layoff, they get over it, admit it happened, but then show up full of enthusiasm to try something new at a list of companies that they really would like working for, often for job slots that will be a new and exciting challenge.

When a storm rolls in, the water skiers pull their boat out of the water, pack it up, and head home. The hard-core surfers on the other hand, paddle out into the ocean, knowing that new, bigger waves are coming soon.

The lesson is simple but profound. Change will absolutely happen, often. You must decide that change is good and that it offers opportunity for you. You must decide to be flexible. You must adopt an inner formula of accept, understand, adapt, and overcome. You must find the right mentors and advisors who will help you in this regard, not naysayers that always default to stick it out no matter how bad things are getting. If a job is degrading, the signs are usually obvious, yet often only one person on the team starts putting his resume out and looking for better scenarios. Be that person who develops great awareness and seeks better opportunities proactively.

I made this mistake after founding a smartphone software company. My co-founder and I were early and right, presciently predicting the future growth of the BlackBerry. We created what easily became the best task management system for the BlackBerry, enjoyed marketing success, and rode the wave as BlackBerry as the platform went from 400,000 users in 2004 to 50,000,000 in 2011. Our revenues were doubling every two months, we added good people, and we created several additional well-regarded apps that sold well, even as Steve Jobs revealed the iPhone in 2007.

Apple then opened the iPhone to developers in 2008, but the first apps were all tiny little apps that did next to nothing for 99 cents. Few serious business users were defecting to the iPhone because the BlackBerry was just so much better a tool for getting important work done. We continued to waterski on our BlackBerry Lake but the storm clouds were forming. By early 2009, we were working in earnest to rewrite our apps for the iPhone, but it was too late when we finally released on iOS in 2010. The Apple wave had already risen from the ocean, and we missed it. The developers who started on Apple had a huge lead and although the task management apps that initially came out for the iPhone only offered 1/10th of what our apps could do, it didn't matter. We couldn't move up the AppStore list and the wave passed us by.

We were not flexible enough and didn't pivot fast enough. The company was our baby. The BlackBerry market continued to succeed for a while through 2010 and 2011, even though the writing was on the wall. Our core market — high-end executives and knowledge workers — defected from BlackBerry at astounding rates in 2010 and 2011, even as a different group bought more BlackBerry devices. Apple was growing in sophistication and so were the third-party apps. Google released Android in late 2008, and that wave started to grow, even though Android looked like a total sh*t show mess at the time. Never under-appreciate the power of "free" when big players like Samsung want in. We were not big enough to fight on three fronts at once, and our skill set was best fit for the BlackBerry.

We held on through 2012, wasting money as losses mounted and sales fell. The design of the Apple and Google app stores made the game winner takes all: if your app is not in the top 10 - 20 that top a search category, your chances of becoming a sustainable company are poor. We missed both the Apple and Android waves and after eight years, the BlackBerry wave crashed on the rocks and I had to pull the plug.

This lesson applies to careers too. In earlier chapters, we talked about landing in fertile soil at a company that is growing healthily. It was hard to get back in a good employment career situation after a decade of small business ventures, but I decided to tackle that challenge with flexibility and enthusiasm. Managers in an industry tend to hire candidates mostly from environments just like their own because it seems like the safe choice. It was hard, but not impossible. Be flexible, be ready to jump on a new opportunity quickly, and you will improve your odds of top tier success.

I've been surfing again ever since I left BlackBerry Lake. I was surprised when a corporate reduction-in-force got me right after I had crushed my objectives and won the Winners Club trip to Paris. I received the layoff letter the next day after I received the *'congratulations high achiever, you are going to Paris"* letter! The company had decided to simply dump everyone who had been employed less than 5 years with them so that no one could sue for wrongful termination or age discrimination, and I had only been there 4 years. While I was a bit shocked and in truth annoyed because I had my deals lined up to crush numbers again the following year, I didn't hesitate and within three weeks, I had a better position with a much better company and made my numbers in the first year at the new company anyway. In the longer run, the unexpected lay-off was the best thing that could have happened to me. Change worked out for the better.

Be flexible and jump on opportunities quickly when they make sense. Change is constant and those who learn to ride the Banzai Pipeline with abandon enjoy the glory.

We alone determine our own expectations. Many often see expectations as harmless, simple, and inconsequential guesses regarding the future. They are not harmless.

Expectations are incredibly important, more crucial than many realize. They matter, not only in small personal ways but also in organization defining, championship winning, life-and-death ways.

In a small example, imagine you are going to see a movie tonight. You have seen the movie trailers and it looks pretty good. You text your friend that *"we should see 'Last Train to Brooklyn' tonight – I think it looks decent"* and she agrees to go. During the day, you mention your plans to three friends and each one raves about the film. Your expectations rise from 'maybe it will be decent' before going to lunch to 'this is going to be amazing' as the sun dips below the horizon.

Four hours later, you walk out of the theater disappointed. It wasn't a horrible film, but your expectations for near perfection were far greater than the director managed to render at the cineplex. How much more satisfied would you have been if you had not changed your expectations based on comments your friends made during the course of the day?

Off-target expectations happen often in daily life. Imagine the difference between a golfer who expects to shoot one of the best rounds of his life today, versus a golfer who wants to go out to be in the sunshine, to drink a couple of beers, and to hopefully break a 100. Imagine the casual basketball player who heads down to the gym expecting to be the star of the show tonight — even though he rarely is — versus the guy who plans to simply hustle, play good defense, and enjoy seeing his friends. Imagine the person who thinks traffic will be moving quickly, or imagine the person who goes to the restaurant expecting five-star service and the most incredible streak she has ever tasted. Unrealistic, sky-high expectations poison your perception of your experiences.

Expectations matter in bigger contexts too. Expectations often determine what happens next in terms of stock performance and investor patience, they often determine the length of a CEO's tenure, they cause layoffs, and they get people into financial hot water.

Unrealistic expectations cut both ways.

Many people suffer the consequences of limiting expectations. A person who does not expect to get the job, doesn't often get it. A person who doesn't expect to get promoted usually doesn't get promoted. A person who doesn't expect to find the right girl does not look for her or never asks her out. A person who doesn't expect to hit the winning shot, misses badly. So, while it is often smart to set expectations a bit conservatively and to not expect perfection, it is equally important to not set them in a way that limits your destiny.

In some contexts, expectations often determine who lives and who dies. Doctors and nurses see this every day at the hospital's intensive care unit. The person who expects to live, the person who expects to recover, is far more likely to make it than the person who expects that this is, indeed, the end. In the same way, people who expect to stay spry, fun, energetic, enthusiastic, and young-at-heart live fuller lives than those who expect to slow down in retirement as they age.

Expectations play a crucial role in defining the envelope and the upside of your life.

The good news is that you have the power to choose your expectations. Wise expectations set up a positive domino effect that builds momentum. If you become an independent thinker who is not heavily influenced by the opinions of others:

1. You set and control your own expectations.
2. Expectations will then fuel your perceptions and decisions.
3. Your perceptions will absolutely impact your gratitude.
4. Gratitude is the crucial key to daily happiness, and
5. Daily happiness is the secret catalyst which fuels greater success.

There is wisdom in being careful about your expectations, setting them mindfully, and avoiding unrealistic hype. Understanding yourself and striving to beat your own previous bests is far healthier for your psyche than comparing your performance to that of others. Win one game at a time, while deciding what "score" is a winning score. If you become a master at setting accurate, mindful, non-limiting expectations, you will become more optimistic, more positive, more forgiving, happier, a better decision-maker, and ultimately a more grateful and successful human.

Pay attention and be wise with your own expectations.

Chapter 35 | The Ultimate Secret Catalyst

Psychology has made an interesting leap in recent years. After more than 100 years of "modern psychology" studying the human mind for things that go wrong, how to heal people back to normal, and figuring out what average is, the science is finally starting to study why some people dramatically exceed average and achieve outlier success.

There is a prevalent assumption that has limited human potential: Most people believe that if they work hard and become successful, they will then become happy.

In my decades of successes, mistakes, learning lessons, and failing forward, I am certain that the opposite is true: People who are happy, no matter their circumstance, are the ones far more likely to succeed.

The reasons are straightforward. Happy people are more relaxed, see more possibilities, make better social connections, are more optimistic and enthusiastic about their ideas and projects. Their minds are flooded with dopamine which helps them learn and retain information quickly. The ultimate catalyst to success is to be positive and happy most of the time.

But how do you do that?

One key unlocks happiness. It is not money or fame or the weather or any external aspect. The key to happiness is gratefulness. When you are grateful, you notice and appreciate the smallest of things that make your perception of your life better, even when you are feeling challenged or lonely. An incredibly useful habit that will help you notice the good stuff is to write a couple of observations is a "what am I grateful for" journal on a daily basis — whether you decide on a paper journal or simply set up a "journal" email account that you can email your few sentences each day. You don't have to write paragraphs. A simple 200 character "tweet" format will do and helps a lot. Give it a try for 90 days, right after dinner, or better yet, after every meal. Remember that building a good new habit requires a trigger and all of us do eat daily.

Those who live in the present and are truly grateful for every moment, every day, every blessing, every loved one, every little detail, discover that happiness is not a pursuit, but a hidden treasure found within one's own mind.

There is no perfection in this world, so don't expect it. Between occasional big problems and frequent little annoyances, challenging issues dominate our days which can lead to stress, complaints, and unhappiness, if you let them. Media doesn't help. If you listen to the news, the sky is falling, and the world is ending. If you watch your social feeds, it seems like everyone else is living a near perfect, all-too-fun life, and you are missing out most of the time. If you watch the television, Instagram, or YouTube, celebrities are traveling to far away beach resorts, living the secular dream, spending money as fast as they possibly can — and you are not nearly as rich or famous, thinking about your next test grade, or bill to pay, or customer to win, or 10 pounds to lose.

Knowing that the world and people are not perfect, you have a choice to make. You can look for the good nuggets, the silver livings, the lemonade from the lemons, or you can look for the bad nuggets, the flaws, the annoyances. You can avoid a lot of the negativity by deciding what you let into your mind. Every choice is yours and your choices will have a dramatic effect on your happiness and success in the longer run.

If you listen too much to the negative people around you, they are invariably complaining about something all day long, because most haven't realized that they are their own enemy, shooting their own attitude in the foot. It is all too easy to become a lot like the people you associate with most of the time. If you try to solve other people's problems, many times you will find that people don't actually want a solution, and you wind up infecting your own perspective with their negativity. Humans are pre-wired to spend too much time thinking about fears, uncertainties, and doubts — it is part of survival instinct back when we lived in the wilderness surrounded by dangers, but it is not all that helpful now.

This cloud of negativity is exactly why so many stay average, both in success and happiness measures. It offers an extraordinary opportunity for the person who is willing to live large and live positive. You must be comfortable being your independent self, because if you worry about how the crowd judges you, you are sure to bring yourself down. The crowd is — by definition — average, not extraordinary.

The answer is simpler than you might think: figure out what you are grateful for. You don't need 100 friends if you are grateful for the one true friend who you do have. You don't need dozens of Jimmy Choo shoes if you are grateful for that one pair that are just right. You don't need thousands of followers "liking" your posted picture on Instagram, if you are grateful for your sister or one friend who loves you without question. If you are grateful for the smallest of things, from a great t-shirt to a puppy that can't wait to see you, you can be happy. Just don't go shopping too often. Modern shopping is well designed to make you long for things that you don't have. This usually reduces the gratefulness for what you do have. Shopping, so ingrained in the world today, is mostly a drain on happiness.

There are other tactics to improve your happiness. Helping others is near the top of the list, as is learning to only think about and work on stuff that you can personally influence while putting everything else in the hands of God, or, if you prefer, fate. The next time you are feeling blue, volunteer for the weekend and help a charity. I highly recommend reading Shawn Achor's book *The Happiness Advantage* as soon as you have a chance.

To build your gratefulness habit, start your gratitude journal today. Here's an easy way: set up a free email account for just this journal and email yourself notes daily. Make a list of the good relationships, the family that cares for you, the stuff that you love, the freedoms that you have, the goals and memories you cherish, the awesome popsicle you just had, the fact that you live in America and don't have to carry water from a well two miles back to your hut. Email these lists to your journaling account. Being grateful for your blessings is the answer to being happy, day in and day out. It is not a pursuit. Happiness comes from the inside. Thankful people are happy people. Happy people are far more likely to become top 15% people.

I often get asked why I'm so cheerful and happy every day. The answer is simple. I am truly grateful for the little things in life.

Chapter 36 | Competence Required

It is difficult to become top in your field, in your job, in your career, without a top-tier level of competence. Competence is not the same thing as expertise. Experts usually focus on a small, narrow topic and learn it better than 99.8% of the people in similar positions. Competence is knowing the field well, knowing what you don't know, knowing who to contact to find out missing details and answers quickly, and general awareness that is accurate and complete.

People trust competent people. If you bring your car to a mechanic, you expect the mechanic to diagnose it well and give you confidence that he or she can fix it in reasonable time. If you bring your car to a mechanic who says *"gee, I've never seen this issue before and don't even know where to start…"*, your willingness to trust whatever he says next diminishes dramatically.

Unfortunately, in many real-world careers, training is not as good as it could be. New employees are often forced to "fake it until you make it" which is not a great plan. Facing these circumstances, the best move is to quickly ask people for advice, hoping that a few of them turn into good mentors and coaches for you. It pays to have several, because judging the quality of the advice is hard when you have just landed there and sometimes can't tell if the person you are talking to is actually highly competent himself, or just faking it until he makes it.

I hired on to a company which has an extraordinary embarrassment of riches, literally several thousand software products, each one deep and complex. No one employee knows even a quarter of the product line well and specialists roam the halls. In my first week, with zero training, I was asked to go have initial customer meetings on two products I had never heard of. As luck would have it, I had lunch with a director with a decade of experience and he asked me the magic question: *"Have you looked it up on YouTube yet?"* YouTube? He said yes, because other experts want to show off their expertise and YouTube is invariably a treasure trove. I had been trying to find official training materials and was striking out. He laughed at my rookie mistake.

Believe it or not, using Google and other search engines, watching YouTube videos, and reading websites often helps a lot. You will not become an expert from these sources, but you are likely going to be able to learn enough to get through some sticky meetings and conversations. There is a lot to be said for making the effort to educate yourself and not just relying on what the official channels give you. The web has revolutionized how easy access has become, but you must seek if you expect to find.

Many people interviewing for new jobs at new companies don't put in the work, but you can. Anyone who spends three days preparing, inhaling everything that they can find on a company, is likely to impress.

The bottom line is that you must do whatever you can, whatever it takes to build your expertise and competence. In the longer run in a career, there is no faking competence. It often works in the beginning because you have the line *"I've only been here six months..."* in your pocket, but *"I've only been here two years..."* doesn't cut it.

Trust is the number one currency to succeed with people over the long-term. While integrity is the utmost foundation of trust, competence matters too. Average people too often wait for training to come to them while top achievers go and find it. Don't cut corners. Do the work and learn your trade. I have found that it is never brain-surgery difficult, but it does take taking the initiative, having tenacity, and learning every week.

There will be moments in life when the heat is on. It might be the all-important playoff game or a crucial sales meeting. It might be when you are interviewing for a promotion or getting the opportunity to give a talk to an audience of several thousand. These are the moments where you must rise to the challenge with confidence and poise.

How do you do that?

Prepare. Over-prepare. Practice. Greatness flourishes when you are as prepared as possible for the moment, well in advance. Using the public speaking event as an example, present your material many times in advance, in a mirror, on a laptop video, to your friends and mentors. Get constructive criticism. Practice some more.

In sports, Hall of Fame Coach John Wooden had the perfect line for winning basketball: *"Be quick, but don't hurry."* If you hurry your shot, you will probably miss. The idea is to be quick, but to be in control. Many have the will to win, but people who have the will to prepare, to practice, to perfect are the ones that shine on championship day.

As part of preparation, visualization is of utmost importance. Golf legend Arnold Palmer used to visualize his swing and the flight of the ball before every swing. More often than not, the ball mimicked exactly what Arnie had imagined in advance, helping him win 62 PGA Tour titles and seven majors. Visualize yourself giving the presentation flawlessly. Visualize what you will do if you stumble, or if you get interrupted, or if the microphone stops working. People who have mentally prepared and practiced for all scenarios in advance, win.

Ultimately, you must mentally prepare to be at your very best when you face your most challenging moments. You must decide that you can and will rise to the occasion. Every challenge, every battle, is first won in one's own mind.

Some of my biggest personal moments have come in the form of public speaking engagements. I found that getting off to a flawless beginning is an important key to success. If your first sixty seconds command attention and engage the audience, the rest just flows, and overcomes interruptions without derailing the event. To that end, I invest a lot of time trying to design a great opening.

I also learned that the audience may ask questions that have the potential to throw you off track. To overcome that possibility, I think through the top twenty likely questions, and I add material as needed to answer those. Sure, occasionally I get surprised by a curve ball, but if you put your improv hat on, go with the flow, and engage in the conversation, it usually doesn't crater the meeting.

Visualizing how I will handle these exceptions helps me stay calm and confident when things go in a different direction than planned. Visualize smiling and making a little fun of yourself if you get in a flustered situation. People like people who don't take themselves too seriously. Visualize how you will stay confident and recover. Your mind is incredibly powerful and will help you pull it off. If you visualize well, you will execute well.

I strongly suggest watching Amy Cuddy's TED.com speech about the effects of body language and your body's chemical mix, its effect on your confidence, and importantly, a simple hack that will help you become calm under pressure. While not everyone agrees as is always the case in psychology, I truly believe many of her points are valid. Click on escavg.com/amy for a great twenty minutes.

Winning takes confident poise, not frantic panic. Prepare well, practice more than you think that you need to practice, visualize every possible scenario, and you will deliver when the heat is on.

Chapter 38 | Embrace the Good Stuff

When we started this journey together, I started with defining what success means to you. I observed that for most people, just money and fame rarely lead them to a life well lived, a success worth living for.

When I was 22, I was sure that success meant promotions, power, and money. If you ever want to understand the attitude back then, stream the movie 'Wall Street' starring Michael Douglas and Charlie Sheen. I was so sure that I would be CEO of a large corporation someday. What I did not realize at 22 is that real wealth is an incredible mix of different aspects of success, with authentic, loving relationships being far more important than a sprawling house to keep clean.

I have argued that it's a great pursuit to strive to be an outlier, to aim to escape average. Someone is going to be a top percentile success so why not you? But, I truly believe it should not come at the price of relationships.

Love people and help them succeed, for there is plenty of success to go around. More than plenty, actually. Never worry if you will get credit. Love, faith, loyalty, and duty are of utmost importance on the journey that life is. It takes sincere effort and authenticity to invest in fun, lasting relationships, while gaining wisdom and understanding.

To that end, balance matters across a minimum of six dimensions or roles in your life. These roles include your physical and mental health, your spiritual and social connection, your family, and lastly, your work career. For many, there may be additional roles such as community leader, caretaker, and more. A person who is balanced in their approach to life lives a more fulfilling life than one who forgoes everything to win at work alone.

No one, when nearing their final days, wishes that he or she had fewer relationships, fewer people who they loved and were loved in return. No one wishes that they had spent more hours at work, squirreling away more money. It pays to keep the end in mind when you decide what success means to you.

[ESC][AVG] has focused on achievement and becoming a top outlier of success. It is what a lot of people at 22, looking to launch their lives focus on the most. As you get a bit older and wiser, you realize that living a quality life is not the same as just achieving worldly stuff in life.

If you are interested in reading a short book that focuses a bit more on quality of life and less on achievement, I have another book available called *Twenty-One Keys*. *Twenty-One Keys* covers what's missing in the mostly achievement-oriented [ESC][AVG], even though you will find familiar themes as well. True quality in life comes through key pillars such as love, forgiveness, balance, passion, compassion, duty and more. Check out twentyonekeys.com.

Chapter 39 | Why Not You?

Escaping average is a great goal. Once there, you can continue the climb, if you want to, and make it to the top 5%. Making the top 1% stratosphere is possible too, but the top 1% often requires fortunate breaks, more compromises, and less balance in your life. Five out of every one hundred people who you know will achieve this top 5% goal, so why not you?

Step one, bar none, is to find your true north, to know what success you seek, because it is rarely just wealth and fame. Make sure your goals are in writing, with a well thought out 'why' written down each one, and a detailed plan supporting the true #1 goal that you have decided to focus on first. Focus on one great goal at a time and finish that goal, for there is no glory, no accolades, for just starting a race.

The right, best way to set yourself up for this journey is to build the right habits, to practice mental disciplines, until you have rewritten key aspects of your own mental operating system. You have the power to choose in nearly every circumstance, and you have the power to improve in nearly every way. A life well lived is a life where you pushed your own limits and found out what you can become. Don't spend much time comparing yourself to others. It is better to simply focus on getting better than you were yesterday. You can sleep well at night when you know you dared greatly and lived up to your potential.

A background goal that you must have is to become wise beyond your years. The wise never stop learning. They stay curious and ask the right questions with an open mind. Never assume you know, never assume that you understand. [ESC][AVG] offers some ideas but there is more — there is always more. When you seek the "why" that is often hidden from view, you become both wise and a student for life.

Through challenges, remain optimistic and enthusiastic. Look to learn from every setback. Say 'not yet', then adapt and overcome. Embrace people, build trust, have balance, and live large. You can't unread [ESC][AVG] so you now know what it takes, and you know how to get there. All that remains is having the patience and the energy to make it happen.

Acknowledgements

No one has helped me more in my life than my wife, Leslie. She has offered so much encouragement, helping me succeed. I love her with all my heart, and she will always be the center of my universe.

I wrote this book initially for my daughters as they graduated from college. No one could ask for better kids. I can't wait to see how their journeys evolve.

Although they have passed away, I would like to thank my mom and grandparents. A great part of my consciousness is a compilation of the lessons that I learned growing up. I hope your view is great from heaven.

Many of my thoughts and ideas have been inspired by others. Many of those influencers are called out and found on my monthly blog site at optimisman.com. I have tried to refer the reader to several blog posts and resources throughout the [ESC][AVG] book.